Table of Contents

1st printing Nov. 1990, 550 copies
2nd printing May 1991, 1000 copies
3rd printing May 1991, 1000 copies
4th printing June 1991, 1000 copies
5th printing June 1991, 10,000 copies

6th printing July 1991, 10,000 copies
7th printing Aug. 1991, 10,000 copies
8th printing Oct. 1991, 25,000 copies
9th printing Nov. 1991, 25,000 copies

ISBN 0-9631000-0-9

Cover: Thompson's Roller Mill ~ Evening Shade, Arkansas

The Cast of "Evening Shade"

Front row (left to right): Melissa Renee Martin and Jacob Parker.
Second row: Jay R. Ferguson, Ann Wedgeworth, Marilu Henner,
Elizabeth Ashley and Michael Jeter.
Back row: Charles Durning, Burt Reynolds, Hal Holbrook and
Ossie Davis

EVENING SHADE

To All My Friends In Evening Shade,

This extraordinary cookbook, bigger than some but smaller than most, is a valued collection of favorite recipes from some very special people. I can't promise they're all good, but I would venture to say that many will prove to be a memorable experience for your palate. Let's just hope Pepto Bismol won't be the recommended after dinner drink. But more importantly, the proceeds from this cookbook will go towards the construction of a new auditorium-gymnasium at Evening Shade High School, to replace the fifty year old rock structure that currently exists. Not to say that rock buildings are bad, but a regulation size basketball court would provide the Evening Shade ball players an opportunity for more exercise... and a chance to host regulation tournaments.

As my good friend, Virgil, of Ponder's Barbecue Villa says "Keep Your Chin Up" as you try these recipes, because if your chin's down, you'll most likely get food on your shirt.

All the very best and happy cooking!

Burt Reynolds
Coach Wood Newton
"Evening Shade"

According to tradition... Cherokee Indians, visiting Capt. William Thompson's Mill in the 1820s, called the site "Place of Evening Shade." When the post office was established in 1847, Capt. Thompson made the name official!

EVENING SHADE, ARKANSAS

A Collection of Recipes

Sponsored By

Future Homemakers of America
Evening Shade High School
Evening Shade, Arkansas

Advisor: Mrs. Lita King

Expression of Appreciation

The Evening Shade Future Homemakers of America Chapter would like to thank and express our sincere appreciation to the many people in the community who gave so generously of their time in submitting recipes and assisting with the preparation of our cookbook. Without their help, this book would not have been possible.

The following mothers devoted time and effort in compiling this book: Rena Bowser, Anna Qualls, Joyce Bradford, Virginia Qualls, Cora Lou Davis, and Elizabeth Walker.

Special thanks are extended to the following people: Hillary Rodham Clinton; the producers, cast and crew of the CBS television show "Evening Shade": Linda Bloodworth-Thomason, Harry Thomason, Burt Reynolds, Ossie Davis, Charles Durning, Linda Gehringer, Hal Holbrook, Steve Roth, Dara Monahan, Adrienne Crow, Marilu Henner, Michael Jeter, Elizabeth Ashley, Charlie Dell, Jane Abbott, Burton Gilliam, Jay R. Ferguson, Ann Wedgeworth, Candace Hutson, Jacob Parker, and Loni Anderson.

We also wish to acknowledge Mrs. Eva Haley of Evening Shade, AR and Mr. Craig Ogilvie of Batesville, AR who generously supplied the artwork for our book.

Burt's Friends' Recipes

Spring House ~ Evening Shade, Arkansas

Burt's Beef Stew

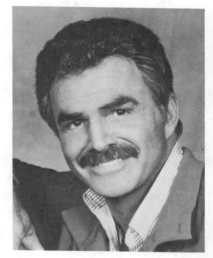

3	slices bacon, cut in small pieces
4	tablespoons flour
1/4	teaspoon pepper
2	pounds lean beef (I like chuck) cut in chunks
1	large onion, chopped
2	cloves garlic, minced
1	28-oz. can tomato sauce
1	cup beef broth
1	cup dry red wine
1	bay leaf (optional)
1	pinch thyme
4	carrots, cut up coarsely
2	stalks celery, cut up coarsely
4	large potatoes, peeled and cut in 4 pieces each
10-12	mushrooms, sliced

In a large pot or Dutch oven, cook bacon until light brown. Combine the flour and pepper in a bowl, dip the meat in the flour mixture to coat completely. Brown in bacon fat, turning often. Add a little vegetable oil if needed. Add onion and garlic and brown them a little.

Add tomato sauce, broth, wine, bay leaf, and thyme. Cover and cook slowly for about 1 1/2 hours. Add carrots, celery, then potatoes and mushrooms. Cook, covered, another 1/2 hour, or until vegetables are tender.

Serve with hot Italian bread, a large salad, fine wine, and good friends.

Linda Bloodworth-Thomason
Executive Producer/Writer
"Evening Shade"
"Designing Women"

Egg Nog

1 quart milk
4 eggs
3/4 cup sugar
1/2 cup bourbon
1 cup cream
Nutmeg

Scald milk: simmer over low heat until a skin appears on top —don't boil! In large bowl, beat eggs until completely smooth. Add sugar, beat together. Remove skin from milk, and pour over eggs/sugar mix. Pour slowly and stir—the hot milk will cook the eggs. Add nutmeg and bourbon to taste. Beat the cream, and fold in. Refrigerate.

Harry Thomason
Executive Producer/Director
"Evening Shade"
"Designing Women"

Chicken Masala

2-3 boneless chicken breasts (skinned)
6-8 mushrooms
6 scallions
1 1/2 tablespoons butter or margarine
1 cup white wine
1 cup grated cheddar cheese
2 cloves garlic
Basil
Flour

In a large skillet melt butter. Chop and saute mushrooms. Chop and add scallions (white/light green parts only). Cut chicken breasts in half, roll in flour, and add to skillet. Pour in wine. Add garlic and basil to taste. Cook over moderate heat 4-6 minutes, turn chicken breasts, cook until done. Sprinkle grated cheese over chicken, remove skillet from heat, and cover dish until cheese melts.
Serve with rice.

"Ponder Blue"
Ossie Davis

"I'm an eater, not a cook; my skills do not come into play until the dinner bell rings. My only recipe is how to kiss the chef when the meal is over".

"Dr. Harlan Eldridge"
Charles Durning

Spanish Rice

Saute in oil - chopped onion, chopped green pepper, chopped celery. When partially cooked, add chopped meat, sliced fresh mushrooms and cook until meat loses red color. Add large can of tomatoes, small can of tomato sauce, a few whole cloves, bay leaf, salt and pepper.

Simmer 1/2 hour. Meantime, par boil 1 cup of rice.
Mix rice and sauce and put in greased cassserole dish. sprinkle with Parmesan cheese and bake at 375 degrees about 30 minutes, until bubbly. Remove bay leaf and cloves after its cooked. Serve with rolls and salad.

Mary Ann & Charles Durning

"Evan Evans"
Hal Holbrook's Favorite Recipe
for Salad Dressing

Wash and dry lettuce
Pour plenty of Extra Virgin Olive Oil (green) on it
Toss lightly
Shake on herbs marked "Salad Herbs" and "Cilantro", and salt and pepper to taste.
Toss again.

"Fontana Beausoleil"
Linda Gehringer

"I've never been much of a cook, so years ago when I was asked to bring a "dish", I would always show up with the delicious Brownies and everyone would ask for the recipe and I'd just smile and say I couldn't tell. The secret being they came from a box - I just helped dress them up a bit."

1 box Family Size Duncan Hines Double Fudge Brownie Mix
1-6 ounce package Nestles Chocolate Chips
4 ounces sliced Almonds or Chopped Pecans

In a 9x13 pan sprinkle the chocolate chips and nuts over the prepared Brownie Mix and cook according to package directions. Be careful not to overcook - if anything 'undercook' and then let them cool for at least an hour before you cut them in 2 inch squares (or 3 inch to be really impressive). And if anyone asks you where you got the recipe just smile and say it's a secret.

"Ava Newton"
Marilu Henner

Vegetable Pate II (French)

Squash layer
1 butternut squash (about 1 1/2 to 2 lbs.)
2 Tbsp. butter or margarine   2 Tbsp. flour
1/4 cup half-and-half   1/2 tsp. salt
1/4 tsp. ground cinnamon
1/4 tsp. ground ginger   2 eggs, lightly beaten

Mushroom layer
1/4 cup butter or margarine
1 lb. mushrooms, finely chopped (4 cups)
1 large onion, finely chopped (1 cup)   1 tsp. salt
1/4 tsp. freshly ground black pepper
2 eggs, lightly beaten
1/4 cup packaged bread crumbs

Broccoli layer
2 pkgs. (10 oz. each) frozen chopped broccoli   2 Tbsp. butter or margarine
1 medium-size onion, finely chopped (1/2 cup)   1 clove garlic, finely chopped
1/2 cup half-and-half   3 eggs   1/4 cup packaged bread crumbs
1/4 cup (1 oz.) freshly grated Parmesan   1/8 tsp. ground nutmeg   1/2 tsp. salt

1. Peel and cut the squash into cubes and place in a large saucepan. Cover with boiling salted water and return to boil. Cover and simmer until very tender, about 30 minutes. Drain and puree in the container of an electric blender or a food processor. **2.** In a medium saucepan melt the butter, stir in flour, half-and-half, salt, squash, cinnamon and ginger. Cook, stirring, until mixture thickens and bubbles. Remove from heat and stir in the eggs. Turn into a greased 9x5x3 inch loaf pan lined on the bottom and sides with foil. **3.** Heat the butter and saute the mushrooms and onion until tender and most of the moisture has evaporated. Off the heat stir in salt, pepper, eggs and bread crumbs. Place on top of squash mixture. **4.** Cook the broccoli according to package directions. Drain and chop finely. Place in bowl. **5.** Meanwhile heat the butter in a small saucepan and saute the onion until tender but not browned. Add garlic and cook 1 minute. Add to broccoli. **6.** Preheat over to 350 degrees. Add half-and-half, eggs, bread crumbs, cheese, nutmeg, and salt to broccoli. Mix well and place on top of mushroom mixture. Place loaf pan in a 13x9x2 inch baking pan in the middle of the oven. Pour boiling water into outer pan to a depth of about 2 inches. Bake at 350 degrees for 2 hours or until pate is set. Remove loaf pan to a wire rack to cool. Chill several hours or overnight. **7.** Unmold onto a platter and garnish with watercress, if you wish.

"Herman Stiles"
Michael Jeter

Anything from: TUTTOBENE
                905 N. Fairfax Avenue
                West Hollywood, CA 90046

Sorry. I can't cook!
Michael Jeter

"Aunt Freida Evans"
Elizabeth Ashley

Upside Down Cocoa Cake
1 heaping cup flour
3/4 cup sugar
1 1/2 Tbsp. cocoa
2 tsp. baking powder
3/4 tsp. salt

Sift all together and add to:
1/2 cup milk
2 Tbsp. melted butter
1 tsp. vanilla
Put in 8 inch greased pan.

Make syrup to be poured over batter.
1/2 cup brown sugar
1/2 cup granulated sugar
1 cup hot water
2 Tbsp. cocoa
Boil 5 minutes and pour over batter. Bake 350 degrees for 40 minutes.

"Nub Oliver"
Charlie Dell
Nub Oliver's Armadillo Eggs
20 whole jalapeno peppers (2 jars, usually)
1 pound Monterrey, cheddar or jack cheese, shredded
1 pound of uncooked hot sausage
1 cup Bisquick
This is Nub's favorite thing to fix for appetizers. He likes to start the social occasion off to a rousing start. That's why in private he calls this his "Fanny Surprises". You'll see why because they're very hot! Firecracker HOT!!
To start, you split and remove the seeds from the jalapenos. When you split them, don't cut them in two. Leave them intact. (When Nub does this, he always likes to wear gloves when he deseeds his jalapenos 'cause these little fellers are hot.) Then you stuff them with your shredded cheese of choice. This takes 1/2 pound of the cheese. Then close the jalapenos back together. A little cheese may hang out, but that's okay. In a separate bowl, mix together the 1 pound of uncooked hot sausage, 1 cup of Bisquick and the other 1/2 pound of shredded cheese. Take this mixture and roll or pat it around the stuffed jalapenos to make an egg shape. Then put them on an ungreased cookie sheet and bake at 350 degrees for 25 minutes or until they look done (usually a little brown).

"Dorothy"
Jane Abbott

I stole this from my mother - who probably got it from my Aunt Lilly - who probably got it from my Aunt Bette - who probably got it from a good ole southern cookbook!
Anyway - it's a simple dish to make and it's yummy!!!

Garlic Cheese Grits

1 cup grits	1 roll (6 ozs.) garlic cheese
1/2 cup butter or oleo	3 eggs
2/3 cup milk	1/2 cup grated cheddar cheese

Cook grits (according to directions on the box). Add the garlic cheese and butter. Cool. Add eggs and milk. Pour into a greased casserole pan and bake at 350 degrees for about 30-35 minutes. Put grated cheese on top and bake another 10 minutes until cheese melts. Serves enough for a table of bridge players!

"Virgil"
Burton Gilliam

Two Alarm Chili

1 package of Wick Fowler's Two Alarm Chili Seasoning Mix
1 1/2 lbs. ground chuck or chili meat
2 cans tomato sauce
1 can whole tomatoes
1 diced onion
1/2 cup grated cheddar cheese
Pace Picante Sauce

Brown meat and onions. Follow the directions on the seasoning mix. Top with cheese and picante sauce. (Hot sauce and jalapenos optional.)

"Taylor Newton"
Jay R. Ferguson

This is my Grandmother's recipe. My mom taught me how to make it. I love it!

Doty Gammel's Sweet Potato Souffle with Topping

2 cups mashed sweet potatoes
1 1/4 cups sugar
2 eggs   3/4 stick oleo
1 cup milk   1/2 tsp. cinnamon
1/2 tsp. nutmeg

Mix all ingredients into mashed potatoes. Pour into casserole and bake in 400 degree oven for 20 minutes. Sprinkle topping evenly over potatoes and continue baking 10 minutes.
Topping: Melt 3/4 stick oleo or butter. Mix in 3/4 cups crushed corn flakes, 1/2 cup chopped nuts, 1/2 cup brown sugar.

"Merleen Eldridge"
Ann Wedgeworth

Fruit Cocktail Cake

1 1/2 cups sugar
2 cups flour
2 tsp. soda
2 eggs, well beaten
1 #303 can fruit cocktail

Mix and pour in greased pan. Sprinkle 1/2 cup brown sugar and 1/2 cup nuts mixture on top of cake. Bake at 350 degrees about 30 minutes.

Icing

Melt 1 stick margarine, add 3/4 cups sugar, 1 cup coconut
3/4 cup Pet milk (no substitute)
1/2 tsp. vanilla
Boil 2 minutes and pour over cake while still hot. Put nuts on top.

"Molly Newton"
Candace Hutson

Chocolate Chip Cookies are my favorite cookies. Just follow the recipe on the package! Serve with chocolate milk.

"Will Newton"
Jacob Parker

Jacob invites his buddies over for a few of his favorites!

Peanut Butter and Jelly Sandwich

Wheat Bread - 2 slices
Jiffy creamy peanut butter
Grape Jam

Spread peanut butter on one piece of bread. Spread jam on the other piece of bread. Put together and cut in half.

Artichoke with Butter Sauce

Boil one artichoke until tender, about 20 minutes.

Sauce:

1 cup butter, melted   garlic powder to season
1 to 2 Tbsp. of real lemon juice
Heat until boiling. Dip artichoke in butter sauce and fight over the heart...

Hillary Rodham Clinton
First Lady, State of Arkansas

Chicken and Rice Deluxe

2 T. Butter	2 T. chopped green pepper
	2 T. chopped onion
	2 cups cooked chicken, cut into bite-sized pieces
	1 (6 oz.) package wild rice or long grain and wild rice, cooked
	1/2 cup mayonnaise
	1 (6 oz.) can French style green beans, drained
	1 (10 3/4 oz.) can cream of celery soup
	1/2 cup sliced water chestnuts
1/4 tsp. salt	Pepper to taste
	Juice of 1 lemon
	1 cup grated cheddar cheese

Saute green pepper and onion in 2 tablespoons butter. Combine all ingredients and place in a greased 2 quart casserole dish. Bake at 350°, uncovered, for 25 to 30 minutes. Top with grated cheese and cook 5 more minutes or until cheese is melted.

Loni Anderson
Mrs. Burt Reynolds

Company Cheesecake

1 1/4 cups graham cracker crumbs
2 Tbsp. sugar   3 Tbsp. butter or margarine, melted
2 packages (8 oz. each)
plus 1 package (3 oz.) cream cheese, softened
2 tsp. grated lemon peel (or lemon juice)
1 cup sugar   1/4 tsp. vanilla   3 eggs
1 cup dairy sour cream or Strawberry Glaze

Heat oven to 350 degrees. Stir together cracker crumbs and 2 Tbsp. sugar. Mix in butter thoroughly. Press mixture evenly in bottom of 9-inch springform pan. Bake 10 minutes. Cool. Reduce oven temperature to 300 degrees. Beat cream cheese in large mixer bowl. Gradually add 1 cup sugar, beat until fluffy. Add lemon peel and vanilla. Beat in eggs, one at a time. Pour over crumb mixture. Bake 1 hour or until center is firm. Cool to room temperature. Spread with sour cream or glaze. Chill at least 3 hours. Loosen edge of cheesecake with knife before removing side of pan. Serves 12.

Strawberry Glaze

Mash enough fresh strawberries to measure 1 cup. Blend 1 cup sugar and 3 Tbsp. cornstarch in small saucepan. Stir in 1/3 cup water and the strawberries. Cook, stirring constantly, until mixture thickens and boils. Boil and stir 1 minute. Cool thoroughly.

Steve Roth
Personal Assistant to Linda Bloodworth-Thomason

Sunshine Salad

2 cups shredded carrots
1 cup shredded coconut
2 cans mandarin oranges
2 cups raisins
2 cups sunflower seeds
2 lemon or orange yogurt (small size)

Combine all ingredients. Add more or less of each ingredient according to personal taste. Makes a large bowl of healthy, tasty salad for picnic or occasion.

Adrienne Crow
Administrative Assistant
Mozark Productions

Blueberry Freezer Jam

4 cups blueberries
2 cups sugar
1 small package lemon gelatin

In large pot crush 2 cups of berries. Pour in remaining berries, sugar and gelatin. Bring to a boil; boil for two minutes. Ladle into freezer containers or jars; let cool and freeze. Try this with other fruits. For example, 4 cups strawberries or raspberries, 2 cups sugar, 1 package strawberry gelatin, or 6 cups peeled, chopped peaches with juice, 2 1/2 cups sugar, and 2 packages of peach gelatin.

Dara Monahan
Executive Assistant
Mozark Productions

New York Egg Cream (Drink)

12 oz. soda water
3 tsps. chocolate syrup
4 oz. milk

Pour soda water into a 16-oz. glass (frosted, if possible). Add chocolate syrup and stir. Add milk slowly and stir.

Appetizers and Beverages

Spring House ~ Evening Shade, Arkansas

Appetizer Tortilla Pinwheels

Filling:

    8 ozs. dairy sour cream
    1 pkg. (8 ozs.) cream cheese, softened
    1 can (4 ozs.) diced green chillies, well drained
    1 can (4 ozs.) chopped black olives, well drained
    1 c. grated cheddar cheese   1/2 cup chopped green onions
    Garlic powder to taste   Seasoned salt to taste

Other ingredients:

    5 (10 inch) flour tortillas   Fresh parsley for garnish
    Salsa

Mix all of the filling ingredients together thoroughly. Divide the filling and spread evenly over the tortillas; roll up tortillas. Cover tightly with plastic wrap twisting ends. Refrigerate for several hours. Unwrap. Cut in 1/2 inch slices. An electric knife is best. Discard ends. Lay pinwheels on serving plate and garnish with parsley. Leave space in center for small bowl of salsa if desired.

Yield: About 50

Berneice Haley

Caramel Nut Crunch

    48 graham crackers
    1 cup butter
    1 cup brown sugar
    1 cup nuts (chopped)

Cover jelly roll pan with foil; preheat oven 350 degrees. Fill pan with individual graham crackers, side by side. Combine and boil sugar and butter; then add nuts and spread over crackers. Bake 10 minutes. Cut while warm. Store in air tight container

Joey Smith

Cheese Balls

    2 - 8 oz. packages cream cheese, softened
    2 teaspoons chopped onion
    1/4 cup finely chopped green pepper
    1 - 8 oz. can crushed pineapple, drained
    1 tsp. seasoning salt

Mix together and chill. Shape as desired and roll in chopped pecans or walnuts.

Mona Ray

Cheese Roll

    1 jar Old English Cheese Spread   1 jar Bacon Cheese Spread
    1 8 oz. cream cheese   1 tbsp. parsley flakes

Let cheese soften at room temperature. Mix and refrigerate. Use shortening to grease hands. Form into a ball. Roll in 1 cup chopped pecans and serve with your favorite crackers.

Cindy Binder

Cocktail Wieners

Mix one 6-ounce jar (3/4 cup) prepared mustard and one 10-ounce jar (one cup) currant jelly in chafing dish or saucepan on low heat. Slice 1 pound (8 to 10) frankfurters diagonally in bite-size pieces. Add to sauce and heat through. Serve hot.

Rena Bowser

Deviled Ham Puffs

1 - 8 oz. pkg. cream cheese
1/4 tsp. onion salt
1 - 4-1/2 oz. can deviled ham

1/4 tsp. baking powder
1 egg yolk
crackers or baked toast

Mix all ingredients together well. Place in a pastry bag with large star tube and squeeze onto toast or crackers. If pastry bag is not available, use teaspoon and dab a small amount on toast or crackers. Broil for 5 to 8 minutes or until puffy; serve immediately! These may be prepared in advance and refrigerated until ready to broil. Crackers might become soggy, but will become crisp again in the oven. Makes around 20 - 24.

Eleanor Yager

Olive Appetizer

1 box Ritz crackers
1 jar of cheese whiz Jalapeno Spread
1 jar of olives   1 box toothpicks

Take 1 ritz cracker and cover with cheese spread. Stick a toothpick through an olive and put it on the cracker. Make as many as you need.

JoAnn Flynn

Pizza Treats

Ingredients needed: Bread, American cheese (as many slices as you have bread), sausage, and tomato sauce.

Toast bread; cut into four equal squares. Spread tomato sauce on bread. Cut cheese into four equal squares. Put each square on one square of bread. Fry sausage. Sprinkle sausage on bread and cheese. Heat in microwave until cheese bubbles.

Clay Smith

2

Porcupine Meat Balls

1 1/2 lbs. ground beef
1 tsp. salt
1 tsp. onion, minced
1/2 cup water

1/2 cup rice
1/2 tsp. pepper
1 small can tomato soup

Wash rice; combine with meat, salt, pepper, and onion. Shape into balls and place in shallow baking dish in a single layer. Heat soup and water, and pour over meat balls. Bake at 325 degrees for 1 1/2 hours. Serves 6 - 8

Steven Burkhart

Sausage Balls

1 lb. hot sausage
3 cups Bisquick

10 ozs. sharp cheddar cheese

Grate cheese. Mix sausage and bisquick. Shape into one inch balls. Bake 20 minutes - 375 degrees.

Deltha Sharp

Spiced Up Rotel Dip Sauce

2 lb. velveeta cheese
1/2 lb. sausage

1 can diced Rotel tomatoes
2 tablespoons chili powder

Brown sausage in skillet and drain off excess cooking fat. In double boiler or if using microwave heat Rotel tomatoes until hot; add cheese and heat until melted. Add chili powder and cooked sausage. For thicker dip use more cheese. Serve with chips or over cooked vegetables.

Wanda Kunkel

Spicy Party Dip

1 - 18 oz. jar Picante Sauce (mild or hot)
1 - 16 oz. sour cream
1/2 moon longhorn colby cheese, shredded
1 - 6 oz. can olives, pitted and sliced

Spread sour cream onto a large cookie sheet. Alternate layers of picante sauce and shredded cheese. Top with sliced black olives.
Refrigerate for at least one hour. Serve with your favorite tortilla or corn chips.

Sondra Williams

Cherry Punch

1 pkg. cherry-flavored gelatin
4 tablespoons sugar
3 cups water
1/2 bottle gingerale

1 pint hot water
1/8 teaspoon salt
6 tablespoons lemon juice

Dissolve gelatin in hot water. Add sugar and salt and stir until dissolved. Add water, lemon juice, and gingerale. Pour over ice.

Serves 6

Geraldine Kunkel

Cranberry Orange Cooler

1 pkg. (4 serving size) Jello brand gelatin, orange flavor
1 c. boiling water
ice cubes

2 1/2 c. cranberry juice, chilled
orange slices

Dissolve gelatin in boiling water. Add cranberry juice. Pour over ice cubes in tall glasses and garnish with orange slices if desired. Makes about 3 1/2 cups.

Alisa Arnold

Easy Pudding Milkshakes

3 c. cold milk
1 pkg. Jello instant pudding and pie filling, any flavor
1 1/2 c. ice cream, any flavor

Pour milk into blender; add pudding mix and ice cream; cover. Blend at high speed 30 seconds until smooth. Pour into glasses.

Alisa Arnold

Easy Punch

6 c. pineapple juice
3 qts. gingerale (or sprite)
1 1/2 gallons sherbet (orange or pineapple)

3 c. orange juice

Combine. Float the sherbet on top.

Leta Engle

Golden Punch

2 - 6 oz. cans frozen orange juice
2 qts. gingerale
3 trays crushed ice

1 1/2 c. white Karo
1 qt. sherbet (orange)

Empty juice and Karo into punch bowl. Add sherbet and ice; pour gingerale over the mixture. Allow most of the ice to melt. Thin slices of oranges may be floated on top.

Leta Engle

Hot Chocolate Mix

1 - 25.6 oz. box non-fat dry milk   1 - 6 oz. jar instant creamer
2 c. powdered sugar   1 - 16 oz. chocolate drink mix
1 large box instant pudding
Mix all together. Use 3 spoons per cup; add boiling water.

Leta Engle

Red Punch

1 pkg. strawberry koolaid   1 pkg. cherry koolaid
2 c. sugar   8 c. water
1 pt. pineapple juice   1 pt. gingerale
Mix everything except gingerale together and chill. Add chilled gingerale just before serving.

Elizabeth Walker

Tea Sparkle

6 tea bags   3 c. boiling water
28 ozs. lemon-lime carbonated beverage
Prepare tea and cool to room temperature. Stir in carbonated beverage.

Lita King

5

Perfect Party Pleasers

Cheese and fruit tasting is an easy, conversation-making way to entertain friends before dinner. Seasonal varieties of fruit include peaches, nectarines, sweet cherries, figs, grapes, apricots, pineapple, strawberries, plums and melons. Or try fruits such as papaya and mangoes. Dried fruits such as prunes and raisins also team nicely with cheese and fresh fruits.

Some cheese and fruit combinations: Cheddar, Provolone and Camembert with pineapple, grapes, pears and walnuts. Brie, Monterey Jack and Feta with tangerines, strawberries and dried prunes. Colby, Gjetost, Emmenthaler and Roquefort with apricots, pineapple and plums.

Remember, if cooking the cheese for your appetizers, that excessive heat and prolonged cooking turns it stringy and leathery. When making a sauce, stir in the cheese toward the end of cooking time just until totally melted.

To keep egg yolks from crumbling when slicing hard cooked eggs, wet the knife before each cut.

The pointed end of a beer can opener is an excellent tool for deveining shrimp.

Out of ginger ale? Mix equal parts of Coke and 7-Up.

Use styrofoam egg cartons as trays when you need extra ice cubes for parties.

If the carbonation fizzes out of your champagne, add one raisin to the bottle. The raisin won't affect the taste but its raw sugar will start the bubbling up again.

Christmas Starter, dinner or breakfast: Serve Cranberry Juice topped with lime sherbet.

You can use frozen dough to make flaky crusts for appetizers. Thaw, cut into desired shapes, put in filling, brush with butter, bake 10-15 minutes at 375 degrees. Fillings can be chopped up chicken, roast beef or any cooked seafood; or any cooked vegetables as mushrooms, broccoli, cauliflower.

Place a bay leaf (which are never to be eaten) in a tea ball for easy removal from sauces (or stews).

For instant white sauce: blend together 1 c. soft butter and 1 c. flour. Spread in an ice cube tray, chill well, cut into 16 cubes before storing in a plastic bag in the freezer. For medium-thick sauce: drop 1 cube into 1 c. of milk and heat slowly, stirring as it thickens.

Store carton of cottage cheese upside down. It will keep twice as long.

Soups, Salads and Vegetables

Spring House ~ Evening Shade, Arkansas

Angel Salad

1 pkg. lime Jello   1/4 cup sugar
1 cup boiling water (use part pineapple juice)

Cool until it begins to thicken. Add 1 cup marshmallows (cut fine). Add 1 small pkg. philadelphia cream cheese, 1 cup (small can) crushed drained pineapple, 1/2 cup nuts, juice of 1/2 lemon, 1/2 pt. whipped cream.

Elizabeth Walker

Baked Beans

1 med. onion
1/2 lb. bacon cut into bite sized pieces
6 cans (16 oz.) pork & beans   1/4 cup mustard
1/2 cup ketchup   1-1 1/2 cups brown sugar (pack)

Saute' onion and bacon. Mix with all other ingredients. Place in casserole dish. Bake at 350 degrees for 2-3 hours, until juice is thick. Serves 10-12.

Steve Burkhart

Beef Stew

2 lbs. chuck steaks   2 tbsp. vegetable oil
1 garlic clove, chopped   1 med. onion, chopped
4 ozs. mushrooms, sliced
4 large carrots, peeled and sliced 1/4 inch thick
4 stalks celery, sliced 1/2-inch thick   celery leaves
1 tsp. parsley, chopped   1/2 tsp. oregano
1 tsp. salt   1/2 tsp. pepper
1 1/2 cups water   2 beef bouillon cubes
8 ozs. tomato sauce
6 med. size potatoes, peeled and cubed into 1-inch sizes
16 ozs. frozen peas (or 2 cups fresh)

Remove the excess fat and bones form the chuck steaks and cut them into 1-inch cubes. In a 3-inch deep frying pan, saute' the meat in oil over medium-high heat until browned on all sides (10-15 minutes). Next, add the garlic, onion, and mushrooms and saute' for another 5 minutes, stirring periodically. Last, add the carrots, celery, parsley, and oregano. Season with salt and pepper. Cook over medium-high heat for 10-15 minutes, stirring occasionally. Add about 1 1/2 cups water and the bouillon cubes. After the bouillon cubes dissolve, add the tomato sauce and the potatoes and cook (covered) for about 25 minutes, until the potatoes and meat are tender. Stir often. Continue to add more water as needed to keep the stew juicy. Add the peas during the last 15 minutes of cooking time. Serve hot. Serves 6.

Frank Russo

Broccoli Salad

1 lg. head of broccoli
10 slices bacon, crumbled
1 cup mayonnaise
2 tbsp. vinegar

1/2 cup raisins
1 med. onion, thinly sliced
1/3 cup sugar

Break broccoli into flowerets. In bowl combine broccoli, raisins, bacon, and onion; set aside. For dressing combine mayonnaise, sugar, and vinegar; mix well. Pour over broccoli mixture; chill.

Tammy Brown

Broccoli Salad

2 lbs. broccoli
2 tsp. vinegar
1 tsp. salt
1 lg. garlic clove, finely diced

1/4-1/2 c. vegetable oil
dash oregano
1/2 tsp. pepper

Separate the heads of broccoli into small branchlets, or spears, and remove the excess leaves. Rinse in cold water and drain. Next, in a saucepan, bring 1 cup lightly salted water to a boil. Add the broccoli and cook until tender (about 5 minutes depending on the thickness of the stalks). Do no overcook. Drain the broccoli and place it in a bowl. Last, while the broccoli is still warm, add the oil, vinegar, oregano, salt, pepper, and garlic. Toss the broccoli until well coated with oil, vinegar, and seasonings. Allow the seasonings to mingle for about 10 minutes before serving the salad. Serves 4-6.

Frank Russo

Broccoli - Rice Casserole

1 pkg. frozen broccoli (chopped); cooked and drained
1 can cream of chicken soup
3/4 sticks margarine

1 1/2 c. cooked rice
4 to 6 slices of American cheese

Melt margarine. Combine all ingredients. Pour into 2 qt. baking dish. Bake in 350 degree oven for 30 to 40 minutes, uncovered.

Natalie Smith

Broccoli - Rice Casserole

1 c. rice
1 sm. jar of cheese whiz
1/2 c. chopped celery
1 pkg. chopped broccoli (frozen)

1 can mushroom soup
1/2 c. chopped onion
1/4 stick margarine

Cook rice; add soup and cheese. Saute' onions and celery in margarine. Thaw broccoli with hot water. Drain and mix broccoli with other ingredients. Put in baking dish and bake at 325 degrees for 45 minutes.

Chicken Soup

1 sm. onion chopped	1 lg. garlic clove finely chopped
3 carrots	3 potatoes
3 celery stalks	2 cans cream of chicken soup
1-8 oz. pkg. of egg noodles	

Boil chicken in 1-2 qts. of water. Add onion and garlic to chicken; boil until chicken comes off the bone easily. In separate pan cook carrots and celery until tender; drain. Add carrots, celery, potatoes, and cream of chicken soup to both; let simmer to cook potatoes while noodles cook. Prepare noodles as directed on package. Add to soup.

Linda Taylor

Christmas Salad

1-6 oz. pkg. lime Jello	1 c. boiling water
1 c. miracle whip	1 c. chopped pecans
1-16 oz. can crushed pineapple, drained	
12 ozs. cottage cheese	
1 lg. can evaporated milk, chilled to whip	

Dissolve jello in boiling water. Add cottage cheese, pineapple, pecans and miracle whip. Mix well. Whip evaporated milk until stiff. Fold whipped milk into the jello mixture. Pour into molds and refrigerate. Stores well, covered. Recipe can be divided in half.

Wilma Rogers

Clam Chowder

1 can cream of potato soup	1 can cream of celery soup
1 can cream of mushroom soup	1 qt. 1/2 & 1/2 cream
1 can New England clam chowder	1 can mushrooms
1 can minced clams	1 stick oleo

Heat and serve. (Do not let mixture boil. Also is better after it sets over night)

Connie Boyle

Classic Potato Salad

1 c. mayonnaise	2 tbsp. vinegar
1 1/2 tsp. salt	1 tsp. pepper
4 c. cooked, peeled, cubed potatoes	1 c. sliced celery
1/2 c. chopped onion	2 hard-cooked eggs, chopped

In large bowl, stir together first 5 ingredients; until smooth. Add remaining ingredients; toss to coat well. Cover and chill. Makes 5 cups.

Lola Flynn

Cornbread Salad

12 oz. cornbread mix
1 small onion, chopped
1 c. whole kernel corn, drained
1 c. cubed ham
1 pint buttermilk salad dressing

1 green pepper, chopped
1 ripe tomato, chopped
3 hard cooked eggs, chopped
1/4 tsp. salt

Bake cornbread according to package directions. Cool and break into pieces in large salad bowl. Add remaining ingredients, toss and chill for 2 hours or longer before serving.

Connie Boyle

Corn Casserole

1 can cream style corn
1 egg
1 med. green pepper
2/3 c. milk
1 c. grated sharp cheese or cheese of your choice.
1/4 cup melted margarine
Salt & pepper to taste

1 can whole kernel corn
1 lg. chopped onion
1 sm. jar pimentos
1 c. cracker crumbs

1 1/4 tbsp. sugar
Paprika (optional)

Combine ingredients and place in greased dish. Cook at 350 degrees for 45 minutes to 1 hr.

Mary King

Curried Ham Salad

2 c. uncooked macaroni
1 c. broccoli pieces
1/2 c. mayonnaise
1 1/2 tsp. curry powder
1/2 c. diced celery

3 c. diced ham
1/2 c. french dressing
1 c. cheddar cheese
1/4 tsp. pepper
1/2 c. frozen peas (cooked a bit)

Mix ham and french dressing in a bowl and marinate in the refrigerator. Combine mayonnaise, curry, and pepper. Add to ham with broccoli, celery, peas, and cheese. Cook and rinse macaroni; mix with rest of salad.

Leif Ericson

Easy Garden Vegetable Pie

2 c. chopped fresh broccoli	1/2 c. chopped onions
1/2 c. chopped green peppers	1 1/2 c. milk
1 c. shredded cheddar cheese (about 4 oz.)	
3/4 c. Bisquick baking mix	3 eggs
1 tsp. salt	1/4 tsp. pepper

Heat oven to 400 degrees. Lightly grease pie plate, 10 x 1 1/2 inches. Heat 1 inch salted water (1/2 tsp. salt to 1 c. water) to boiling. Add broccoli. Cover and heat to boiling. Cook until almost tender, about 5 minutes; drain thoroughly. Mix broccoli, onions, green pepper and cheese in pie plate. Beat remaining ingredients until smooth, 15 seconds in blender on high speed or 1 minute with hand beater. Pour into pie plate. Bake until golden brown and knife inserted half way between center and edge comes out clean, 35 to 40 minutes. Let stand 5 minutes before cutting. Garnish as desired. 6 servings.

Cora Lou Davis

Five Cup Salad

1 c. shredded coconut	1 c. miniature marshmallows
1 c. mandarin oranges	1 c. crushed pineapple
1 c. sour cream	

Mix all together. Let stand several hours before serving. Pecans may also be added if desired.

Lola Flynn

French Beans Almondine

2 cans french cut green beans
1/2 lb. bacon (cut into bite sized pieces)
1/2 med. sweet onion (diced)   4-6 oz. slivered almonds

In 2 qt. saucepan, saute' bacon and onion until bacon is lightly browned. Drain 1 can of green beans, and add both cans to bacon-onion mixture. Warm on medium heat until almost ready to serve. Add almonds and warm for 1 more minute. Put in serving bowl and top with a few almond slivers. Serves 6-8.

Steven Burkhart

Fried Eggplant

1 med. eggplant; peel and slice, then soak in salt water for 30 minutes; drain and rinse
    1 egg
    1 c. milk; beat egg with milk in medium bowl
    1 c. corn meal mix   1/2 tsp. salt

Mix salt and meal. Dip eggplant slices in corn meal mix, then in egg and milk mixture, then in corn meal mix again. Fry in deep oil until golden brown. Place on paper towel. Serve while hot.

Cora Lou Davis

Garden Vegetable Casserole

2 sm. yellow summer squash, sliced 1 med. zucchini, sliced
1 sm. white sliced onion 1 sliced tomato
2 tbsp. grated Parmesan cheese 1/2 tsp. seasoned salt
1/2 tsp. basil 1/2 tsp. thyme

Place all sliced vegetables in versatility pan and mix all other ingredients. Toss lightly. Cover and microwave on full power for 8-10 minutes. For conventional oven: Place in oven for 20-25 minutes at 350 degrees.

Joyce Bradford

German Slaw

1 med. head cabbage (shredded) 1 c. sugar (pour over and let set)
Boil: 1 c. vinegar, 1/2 c. oil, 1 tsp. salt, 1 tsp. mustard

Pour over slaw and let set overnight. Green peppers can be added also.

Mickey Avey

Golden Cheese Soup

3 c. chopped potatoes 1 c. water
1/2 c. celery slices 1/2 c. carrot slices
1/4 c. chopped onion 1 tsp. parsley flakes
1 chicken bouillon cube 1/2 tsp. salt
Dash of pepper 1 1/2 c. milk
2 tbsp. flour 1/2 lb. velveeta (cubed)

Simmer above ingredients until tender. Add milk and flour. Stir occasionally until it thickens. Add velveeta.

Elizabeth Walker

Hash Brown Potato Casserole

2 lbs. frozen (southern style) hash browns
1 pt. (16 oz.) sour cream 1 med. chopped onion
2 c. grated velveeta 1 can mushroom soup
Salt & pepper to taste

Put this in 2 small or 1 large casserole dish. Top with:
2 c. crushed corn flakes
1 stick melted parkay (that has been mixed together)

Sprinkle on top of casserole. Bake at 350 degrees for 50 minutes to an hour (depending on thickness).

JoAnn Cushman

Hawaiian Chicken Salad

5 c. diced chicken   1 c. sliced water chestnuts
2 c. chunk pineapple (drained)   1/2 c. chopped celery
1/2 c. chopped onion   1 c. mayonnaise
4 Tbsp. Mayor Grey's chutney (relish)
1/2 c. sour cream   1 tsp. curry powder

Add chinese noodles. Serve on lettuce leaf.

Joyce Bradford

Kidney Bean Salad

1 #300 can Bushes best kidney beans
2 pieces celery, sliced   2 hard cooked eggs, chopped
2 dill pickles, diced   1/4 tsp. salt
1/8 tsp. pepper
1/4 tsp. onion powder or 1/4 c. chopped onion
Mayonnaise or Italian dressing, 4 servings

Drain beans, rinse and drain again. Combine beans with celery, egg, pickle and seasonings. Add mayonnaise.

Lola Flynn

Mom's Vegetable Soup

2 lbs. hamburger meat   2 lg. onions
2 cans whole kernel corn   2 qts. tomato juice
2 lbs. cubed potatoes   1/4 tsp. sugar
Salt & pepper to taste

Brown hamburger. Add onions and cook until clear. Add tomato juice, potatoes, and corn. Mix well. Add sugar, salt, and pepper. Cook at medium heat until potatoes are tender.
Note: Ground deer meat may be substituted for hamburger.

Maleta Engle

Oriental Fried Rice

1/4 c. margarine   1 med. onion, diced
4 eggs beaten   2 cans sliced mushrooms
2 c. Instant rice (follow directions)   1/4 - 1/2 c. soy sauce

Melt margarine in 12" skillet; saute' onions until tender. Then add eggs, scrambled, and brown slightly. Add sliced mushrooms and brown, then add cooked rice. Mix thoroughly, add soy sauce. Yield: 8 1/2 cup servings.

Kathy Haley

Pink Can Salad

2 cans drained pineapple
2 cans eagle brand milk
Pecans

2 cans cherry pie filling
1 lg. Cool Whip

Mix all ingredients and serve.

Lena Herrington

Pork & Bean Salad

2 lb. cans pork and beans in tomato sauce
1/2 lb. bologna, diced
1/2 c. chopped onion
1/4 c. sweet pickle relish
1/8 tsp. pepper

1/2 lb. longhorn cheese, diced
1/4 c. mayonnaise
1/8 tsp. salt

Combine all ingredients in a large bowl; toss gently but thoroughly. Refrigerate for at least 2 hours or overnight. Makes 6 cups.

Lola Flynn

Potato Casserole

6-8 med. potatoes
1 can celery soup (cream)
Salt & pepper to taste

1 can mushroom soup (cream)
1 c. grated cheddar cheese

Peel and dice potatoes. Put into a 2 qt. baking dish. Mix soups and cheese in large mixing bowl; pour over potatoes. Sprinkle with salt and pepper. Cover dish, bake 45 minutes at 350 degrees. Uncover, and bake an extra 15 minutes.

Wanda Kunkel

Potatoes Hashed In Cream

1/4 c. butter
1/2 c. thinly sliced onion
1/4 tsp. black pepper
1 c. undiluted evaporated milk

4 c. cooked diced potatoes
1 tsp. salt
1/2 c. green pepper strips

Melt butter in heavy frying pan; add potatoes, onions, salt and black pepper. Cook over medium heat until potatoes are browned. Add green pepper and milk. Cook until mixture is thick; stir occasionally (about 5-10 minutes). Garnish with pimento strips, if desired. Serve at once. Serves about 6.

Geraldine Kunkel

Royal Rice

1/2 c. finely chopped green onions
3 c. cooked rice (made with beef broth)
1 c. sliced mushrooms

2 tbsp. butter

1 tsp. salt

Saute' onions in butter until tender. Add rice, mushrooms, and salt. Heat thoroughly and fluff with fork. Serves 6.

Lydia Simmons

14

Seven Layer Salad

1 head of lettuce	3/4 c. bell pepper
3/4 c. celery	3/4 c. green onion
1 box frozen green peas	2 c. grated cheddar cheese
1 jar bacon bits	

Layer. Seal with Miracle Whip. Let sit 24 hrs. and toss before serving.

Debbie Stewart

Squash Casserole

1 pkg. corn bread stuffing	1 stick margarine, melted
2 lbs. squash drained	2 sm. raw carrots, grated
1 sm. onion, grated	1 sm. jar pimentos
1 can undiluted cream of chicken soup	
1/2 c. sour cream (optional)	

Mix all ingredients except corn bread stuffing and margarine. Melt margarine and stir into stuffing mix. Use this on top and bottom. Use long glass dish 12 x 8 inches. Bake 30 minutes at 350 degrees.

Anna Lee Little

Sweet Potato Casserole

3 c. mashed cooked sweet potatoes	1/2 c. sugar
1/2 c. brown sugar	1/4 c. milk
1 tsp. vanilla	1 tsp. salt
1 stick oleo	1 c. shredded coconut

Combine all ingredients and place in buttered baking dish. Bake at 350 degrees for 30 minutes.

Topping for above:

1 c. brown sugar	1 stick oleo
1/2 c. flour	1 c. chopped nuts

Combine all ingredients and sprinkle over top of casserole and bake another 15 to 20 minutes.

Gail Barnett

Sweet Potato Honey Balls

2 c. sweet potatoes	Miniature marshmallows, to taste
1 stick butter	1 c. honey

Cook enough sweet potatoes until you have 2 cups. Roll in balls with approximately 5 miniature marshmallows in each ball. Place in pan with 1 stick of melted butter. Pour 1 cup of honey over balls. Bake at 325 degrees for 30 minutes.

Kristie Robison

Three Bean Salad

1 can kidney beans	1 can yellow beans
1 can green beans	1 onion chopped fine
1/3 c. salad oil	3/4 c. sugar
1 tsp. salt	1/2 tsp. pepper

Drain beans; mix well. Let stand over night.

Jean Hamm

Turkey Salad

1 lb. cooked turkey, ground	3 eggs hard boiled
1 c. celery diced	1 tsp. onion minced
1/2 tsp. salt	Pinch white pepper
3/4 c. mayonnaise or salad dressing	1 sm. jar of pimentos (optional)

Mix all ingredients together. Serve on toasted bread or with a lettuce salad and pickle spear. This is a good way to use the leftover turkey from the holidays. It yields 12 1/2 cup servings.

Kathy Holly

Watergate Salad

1 can crushed pineapple	2 pkg. Pistachio instant pudding
1 c. miniature marshmallows	1 lg. container Cool Whip

Mix all ingredients well. Chill for 2 hours. Serve cold.

Raechel McTique

Frog Eye Salad

3/4 cup sugar	1 cup Martha Gooch Acini Di Pepe
1 Tbsp. flour	2 cans (11 oz. ea.) mandarin oranges, drained
1/2 tsp. salt	1 can (20 oz.) chunk pineapple, drained
2/3 cup pineapple juice	1 can (20 oz.) crushed pineapple, drained
1 egg, beaten	1 carton (8 oz.) dairy whipped topping
1 tsp. lemon juice	1 cup miniature marshmallows

In small saucepan mix sugar, flour and salt, stir in pineapple juice and egg. Cook over moderate heat, stirring constantly until thickened. Add lemon juice. Set aside and cool. Cook Acini Di Pepe according to package directions. Combine cooked mixture with Acini Di Pepe. Cover, place in refrigerator until chilled. Combine remaining ingredients, stir lightly, mix with cooked ingredients, serve.

Shalynn Arnold

Main Dishes and Casseroles

Spring House ~ Evening Shade, Arkansas

Club Sandwich

Empty stomach   A working telephone
A delivery menu from Subway sandwich

Call the Subway shop to have home delivery for the delicious "Subway Club Sandwich". Have drinks and chips on hand for a hearty meal.

Connie Grimes

Very Easy Lasagna

Steps:
1. Take carton of frozen lasagna from freezer.
2. Read directions on back of the carton.
3. Follow the directions step by step.
4. Serve with a tossed green salad and your favorite hot bread.

Lula Phillips

All Day Crock Pot Casserole

1 1/2 lbs. ground beef, shaped in patties
2-3 sm. cans pork and beans
5-7 med. potatoes, peeled and sliced thin
1 med. onion, sliced and separated   Salt and pepper to taste
1/4 c. catsup mixed with 1/4 c. water

In crock pot, layer first 5 ingredients, starting with pork and beans, in 3-5 layers of each, ending with pork and beans on top. Pour catsup and water over top, cover, and turn crock pot on high. Place pan under pot in case of overflow. Forget for 6-8 hours. Turn to low for 1 hour. Serve with cornbread. Serves 6-8.

Steve Burkhart

Bacon Casserole

1 lb. bacon   1 (8 oz.) pkg. macaroni
1/2 c. onion (chopped)   3/4 c. sharp cheese (grated)
1 can tomato soup   1 c. milk

Cook macaroni until nearly tender, rinse and drain. (Reserve 4 slices of bacon). Cut remainder in 1/2 inch crosswise pieces. Brown bacon, push to side. Cook onions in drippings until soft. Mix all ingredients and pour into greased casserole. Place bacon slices on top. Bake at 375 degrees for 25 to 30 minutes.

Ann Dienst

Breakfast Pizza

1 lb. sausage
1 c. grated mild cheddar cheese
2 Tbsp. milk
1 pkg. crescent rolls
5 eggs

Brown sausage and drain well. Press out rolls on round pizza pan. Spread sausage, sprinkle cheese then pour beaten eggs and milk over top. Bake at 350 for 25 minutes or until brown.

Cheeseburger Casserole

1 lb. ground beef
1 c. tomato sauce
1/4 tsp. pepper
1 can biscuits
1/4 c. tomato ketchup
1/4 tsp. salt
1 c. onion, chopped
cheese slices

Brown onions and meat; drain. Add salt, pepper, ketchup and tomato sauce. Pour into casserole dish; cover with cheese slices; cover cheese with biscuits. Bake at 350 for 20 to 25 minutes.

Shana Ward

Chili

1 lb. ground beef
1 lg. can tomatoes
1 can kidney beans
2 tsp. basil
1 Tbsp. cooking oil
4 Tbsp. chili powder
1 med. onion
1 6 oz. can tomato paste
2 tsp. minced garlic
1 tsp. salt
Tabasco sauce to desired taste

Brown ground beef and onion in skillet. Drain. In large pot mix tomatoes, tomato paste, garlic, basil, salt, cooking oil, tabasco sauce and chili powder. Bring to boil then turn heat down to simmer. Add beans and meat mixture. Let simmer for 30 minutes. If chili is too thick add desired water before simmering 30 minutes.

Wanda Kunkel

Dianne's Pizza Crust

2 pkgs. yeast
1 1/2 c. flour (self-rising)
3/4 c. hot tap water
1 Tbsp. sugar

Preheat oven to 425 degrees. Dissolve yeast in water. Add sugar and sifted flour. Flour lightly and knead 2 minutes. Let set about 10 minutes to rise. Half dough and roll on floured surface. Shape onto 2 greased pizza pans or 1 large cookie sheet.

Top with your favorite pizza sauce, cheese, and toppings. Bake for 10-12 minutes on middle rack, or until bottom of crust is brown. Makes 2 pizzas.

Sandra Williams

Dinner in a Dish

1 lb. hamburger
1 green pepper
1/4 tsp. pepper
1 can tomatoes
1/2 c. instant rice

1 onion
1 1/2 tsp. salt
1 can whole kernel corn
1 egg

Brown hamburger, onion, green pepper, salt and pepper in skillet and drain. In baking dish mix corn, tomatoes, egg and rice; add meat mixture to baking dish. Top with mozarella cheese. Bake at 350 degrees for 35 to 40 minutes.

Shana Ward

Easy Manicotti

8-10 lasagna noodles
1-15 oz. pkg. Ricotta cheese
2 Tbsp. parsley
1/4 tsp. pepper

8 oz. shredded mozzarella
1/4 c. Parmesan cheese (grated)
1/2 tsp. salt
3 1/2 c. spaghetti sauce (1 jar)

Cook lasagna noodles according to instructions, lay flat and let cool (recommend placing on wax paper while cooling). Mix all other ingredients except spaghetti sauce. When noodles are cool enough to handle, cover each lasagna noodle with cheese mix, pat flat, do not put on too thick, then roll up noodle. In a 9x13 pan put just enough spaghetti sauce to cover bottom, then place rolled up noodles in pan. Cover with remainder of sauce, cover with aluminum foil and bake for 30 minutes at 350 degrees. Some people like more sauce, if so, heat more sauce in pan on stove and serve with manicotti. Makes about 4-5 servings.
Variations: put seafood in with cheese mix or add choice of meat to sauce.

Ann Dienst

Ham and Fruit Kabobs

2 to 2 1/2 lbs. fully cooked boneless ham, cut in 1 1/2-inch cubes
Spiced crab apples
Orange wedges (with peel)
1/3 c. orange marmalade
2 Tbsp. salad oil
1 to 1 1/2 tsp. dry mustard

Quartered pineapple slices
1/2 c. extra hot catsup
2 Tbsp. finely chopped onion
1 Tbsp. lemon juice

Thread ham and fruits alternately on skewers. For sauce, combine remaining ingredients. Broil ham and fruit over slow coals 12 to 15 minutes; brush often with sauce. Use a rotating skewer or turn skewers frequently during broiling. Serves 6.

Rena Bowser

Hamburger and Noodle Casserole

Hamburger meat
1 med. bell pepper
1 Tbsp. salt

2 c. cream of mushroom soup
1 onion
Noodles

Brown hamburger meat, onion and bell pepper. Boil noodles in separate pot; drain water; add 2 cans of soup in large pot. Simmer on low for about 20 to 30 minutes. Then serve.

Lena Herrington

Hobo Beans

1 lg. onion

2 lb. hamburger meat

Cook these two ingredients.
Add: 1 can pinto beans
1 can kidney beans
1 can Rotel
1 tsp. mustard
1 c. ketchup

1 can pork and beans
1 can lima beans
1 c. barbecue sauce
1/2 c. brown sugar

Simmer 45 minutes on stove or 3 to 4 hours in crock pot.

Deanna Strobbe

Ho - Bo Dinner

1 hamburger pattie
1 carrot, peeled and halfed

1 potato, peeled and quartered
1 onion, peeled and quartered

Salt and pepper, to taste. Place all ingredients on aluminum foil (heavy duty kind) seal well; bake at 400 degrees for 1 hour. Each dinner should be wrapped individually if making more than one.

Becky James

Kristie Robison's Quiche

1 c. milk
4 eggs
1/2 c. pepper diced
Salt and pepper

1/2 c. Bisquick
1 lb. meat (ham or bacon)
8 to 10oz. cheese
Vegetables (if desired)

Bake at 450 degrees for 45 minutes or until done.

Kristie Robison

20

Lasagna

8 oz. ribbed lasagna	1 lb. ground beef
1/4 c. chopped onion	1 tsp. salt
1/2 tsp. garlic salt	32 oz. spaghetti sauce

Sm. container of drained cottage cheese

1 lb. shredded mozzarella cheese   1/4 c. Parmesan cheese

Brown ground beef, onion and garlic salt. Add spaghetti sauce and simmer 15 minutes. Cook lasagna according to package. In a greased pan or in casserole dish, layer 3 strips of lasagna. Spread on 1/3 of meat sauce, 1/3 cottage cheese, 1/3 mozzarella. Repeat layering process and top with Parmesan cheese. Bake at 350 degrees for 30 minutes. Let stand 10 minutes before eating. Serves 6 people.

Linda Taylor

Macaroni Pizza

2 c. cooked macaroni	Brown 1 lb. ground beef and one med. onion

Mix and heat the following sauce:

1 can tomato soup	1 can tomato paste
3/4 can water	1 tsp. salt
1/2 tsp. oregano	1/4 tsp. pepper

Beat one egg, 1/2 c. milk and 2 tsp. salt. Grate 1/2 lb. cheddar or mozarella cheese. Layer egg mixture, macaroni, beef, sauce and cheese. Bake in a 9x13 inch pan, greased. Bake at 350 degrees for 20 minutes.

Thelma Paul

Make Ahead Breakfast Sausage and Eggs

6 eggs	2 c. milk
1 tsp. salt	1 lb. bulk sausage

1 c. grated cheddar cheese

6 slices white bread, cubed and crust removed

Brown sausage and pour off grease. Cool and crumble. Beat eggs in mixing bowl. Add milk, salt, cheese, sausage and bread. Pour into greased 8x12 baking dish. Refrigerate overnight. Bake at 350 degrees for 45 minutes or until set. Serves 4 to 6.

Connie Boyle

Meat Loaf

2 lb. hamburger meat	1 med. onion
1 egg	1/2 c. cracker crumbs
1/2 c. ketchup	

Bake at 375 degrees for about 1 1/2 hours.

Sandy Arnold

Mel's Chili

2 lbs. browned ground beef
1 clove garlic squeezed
6 cans water
2 pkgs. Texas chili mix

1 chopped onion
2 cans tomato paste
1 lg. can chili beans

Simmer 2 hours.

Anna Faye Qualls

Mexican Cabbage

2 lb. hamburger
1 bell pepper, chopped
1 tsp. cummin seed
1 can cheddar cheese soup
1 med. cabbage head, shredded

1 lg. onion, chopped
2 cloves garlic, chopped
1 can Rotel
1-16 oz. can tomatoes

Brown first 4 ingredients together in dutch oven; drain off fat. Add soup, Rotel, and tomatoes. Then add salt and pepper to taste and cabbage. Cover and simmer for 45 minutes or until cabbage is done.

Ann Horn

Mexican Skillet

1 lb. sausage
1/2 c. green pepper, diced

1/4 c. onion, diced

Brown sausage in 12" skillet with onions and green pepper. Drain grease from sausage.

Add: 1 c. macaroni uncooked
1 tsp. salt
1-8 oz. can tomato sauce

2 Tbsp. sugar
2 tsp. chili powder
1 1/2 c. water

Stir ingredients, bring to a boil and stir occasionally. Simmer for 10 to 15 minutes, when macaroni are tender add 1/2 c. sour cream and cover with American cheese. Cover to melt cheese. Yield: 8-1/2 c. serving.

Kathy Haley

Mini Meat Loaves and Vegetables

1 1/2 lbs. lean ground beef	1/2 tsp. salt
1 egg	1 can (8 oz.) tomato sauce

1/2 tsp. Durkee Italian Seasoning
1 can (2.8 oz.) Durkee French Fried Onions
6 sm. redskin potatoes, sliced thin
1 bag (16 oz.) frozen broccoli, corn, red pepper combination, thawed and drained

Combine meat, salt, egg, 1/2 can tomato sauce, Italian Seasoning and 1/2 can French Fried Onions. In a 9x14 inch baking dish, form 3 mini loaves. Bake, covered at 375 degrees for 35 minutes. Place vegetables around loaves; stir to combine with the potatoes. Lightly season with salt and pepper, if desired. Top meat loaves with remaining tomato sauce. Bake, uncovered, 15 minutes. Top loaves with remaining onions; bake, uncovered, 5 minutes longer. Makes 3 to 6 servings.

Microwave directions: Prepare meat and potatoes as above except place in an 8x12 inch baking dish and place potatoes under and around meat loaves. Cook, covered, on high 10-13 minutes; turn halfway through cooking time. Add vegetables and top meat with sauce. Cook, covered, on high 7 minutes. Top with remaining onions; cook, uncovered, on high 1 minute. Let stand 5 minutes before serving.

Donna S. Taylor

One & One Casserole

1 lb. ground beef	1 c. uncooked rice
1 c. water	1 can cream of mushroom soup
1 c. sliced green onion tops	1 pkg. onion soup mix

Crumble beef mixture into 2 1/2 qt. casserole pan. Sprinkle with rice and soup. Mix; blend water and mushroom soup, pour over rice. Spread onion tops over mixture; cover casserole. Bake at 350 degrees for 1 hour. Serves 4.

Raechel McTigue

One Pan Pizza

2 c. Bisquick baking mix　　　　2/3 c. milk
2 eggs　　　　　　　　　　　1 c. cut-up pepperoni
1 c. shredded mozzarella cheese (4 oz.)
1/2 c. chopped green pepper　　1/2 c. chopped onion
1 tsp. dried oregano leaves　　1/2 tsp. dried basil leaves
1/2 tsp. garlic powder　　　　1 c. pizza sauce
1 can (4 oz.) mushroom stems and pieces, drained
1 c. shredded mozzarella cheese (4 oz.)

Heat oven to 375. Grease rectangular baking dish, 11x7x11/2 inches. Mix baking mix, milk and eggs in dish with fork until batter is of uniform color (batter will be lumpy). Stir in pepperoni, 1 c. cheese, the green pepper, onion, oregano, basil and garlic powder; spread evenly. Bake until top is light brown, about 30 minutes. Spread with pizza sauce; sprinkle with mushrooms and 1 c. cheese. Bake just until cheese is melted, 1 to 2 minutes longer. 6 servings.

Cheryl Watkins

Pasta Cheese Sauce

1-8 oz. pkg. cream cheese　　1 pt. heavy cream
2 Tbsp. hot water　　　　　2 lbs. pasta (any type)

Cook pasta as directed. Mix cream cheese, cream, water until smooth. Then pour over pasta. Serve with Parmesan cheese to taste.

Raechel McTigue

Pepperoni Spaghetti Bake

8-10 oz. cooked spaghetti noodles　1 c. Prego spaghetti sauce
2-4 oz. sliced mushrooms　　　　　1 sliced bell pepper
About 4 oz. pepperoni
Mozzarella cheese, to taste

In large casserole dish, spread a thin layer of Prego. On this, layer cooked pasta, sauce, green peppers, mushrooms and pepperoni. Continue layers ending with sauce. Then top with generous layer of shredded mozzarella cheese. Bake 350 degrees until cheese turns brown.

Lydia Simmons

Pesto Linguine

5 lg. garlic cloves
1 packed cup fresh parsley, tough stems removed
1 packed cup basil leaves, tough stems removed
1 c. olive oil
1/2 c. grated, good-quality domestic or imported Parmesan cheese
1 lb. thin linguine
4-6 Tbsp. butter

Place the garlic, parsley, and basil in a blender and mix until all the ingredients are finely chopped. Then add the oil and blend for 10-20 seconds. Add the grated cheese and blend for 10-15 seconds longer. Cook the linguine to the al dente stage in rapidly boiling, lightly salted water, according to package instructions. Drain. Add the butter to the hot linguine. Mix in 4-8 tablespoons pesto sauce. If too dry, add a few tablespoons of warm water and/or a few drops of olive oil. Top with additional grated cheese and serve immediately. Serves 4.

Frank Russo

Pork Chops and Rice

6 or more pork chops
1 c. water
3/4 c. chopped bell pepper
1 1/2 tsp. salt

1 c. uncooked rice
3/4 c. chopped onion
2 c. tomato juice
1/2 tsp. pepper

Brown pork chops and lay in bottom of baking dish. Add other ingredients and bake 1 hour at 350 degrees.

Lula Qualls

Rice of Ole'

1 lb. ground beef
1-8 oz. can tomato sauce
1 Tbsp. margarine or meat drippings
1/2 tsp. salt
1/2 c. chopped onion
1 1/2 c. water

1 beef boullion cube

1 Tbsp. chili powder
1/8 tsp. pepper
1/2 c. uncooked rice
1/2 c. cubed cheddar cheese

Brown ground meat and onion in margarine or meat drippings. Add tomato sauce, boullion cube, rice and water. Add salt, pepper and chili powder. Simmer for twenty-five minutes or until rice is done. Add cheese and mix well. Serve immediately.

Luauana Underwood

Seven Layer Casserole

1 c. rice, uncooked
1 chopped onion
Salt and pepper to taste
1/2 cup water
1 c. tomato sauce

1 c. corn (I use green peas too)
1 chopped bell pepper
1/2 cup tomato sauce
3/4 lb. hamburger
3 strips bacon

Arrange the ingredients, except bacon in layers in order given. Lay bacon strips on top. Cover; bake 350 degrees for 1 hour; uncover and bake 30 minutes.

Anna Lee Little

Shipwreck Dish

Layer of chopped onions
Layer of browned hamburger (1 1/2 lb.)
1 c. chopped celery
4 c. tomatoes

Layer of sliced potatoes

1 c. rice
1 c. kidney beans

Do not stir. Cover and bake at 350 degrees for 2 1/2 hours.

Mary Wilson

Skillet Franks and Noodles

1 lb. frankfurters, cut up
1/2 tsp. basil or oregano leaves, crushed
2 Tbsp. butter or margarine
1 can (10 1/2 oz.) condensed cream of celery or mushroom soup
1/2 c. milk
2 c. cooked wide noodles

1/2 c. chopped onion

1/2 c. chopped canned tomatoes
2 Tbsp. chopped parsley

In skillet, brown franks and cook onion with basil in butter until tender. Stir in remaining ingredients. Heat; stir now and then. Serves 4.

Berneice Haley

Skillet Hamburger Casserole

1 lb. ground chuck, ground beef or ground round
1 onion, sliced
1 can whole kernel corn
1 bell pepper, sliced

1 can grean beans
1 can cream of mushroom soup
1 sm. pkg. egg noodles

Salt and pepper to taste. Brown meat, onion, and peppers in electric skillet. Drain off excess fat. Take a potato masher and mash meat mixture; add green beans, corn, soup, plus 1 can water. Simmer on medium heat, salt and pepper to taste; add noodles and 1 can of water - simmer till noodles are tender and until mixture is a creamy texture. Not soupy.
Add grated cheese to top, after cooking and put lid on skillet. Cheese will melt. Serve with salad and rolls.

Becky James

Swedish Meatballs

2 lbs. ground beef
1 tsp. salt
1/4 c. milk
2 eggs
1/4 tsp. nutmeg

1 1/2 c. fine bread crumbs
1 tsp. pepper
1/4 c. applesauce
1 tsp. minced onion

Combine all the above; mix well and form into 48 small balls. Brown in butter, then add water to simmer (about 2 cups). Cook, covered, for around 15 minutes. Serve over rice or noodles. These freeze very well and can also be made smaller to use as hors d'oeuvres.

Eleanor Yagor

Taco Casserole

Nacho cheese chips
Rotel dip
1 lb. brown beef, drained
Lettuce, tomato, and onions, cut up

2 c. cooked rice
1 lb. velveeta cheese
1 c. kidney or brown beans, drained

Place chips in baking dish. Layer browned beef, rice, dip and beans. Place foil over dish so beans won't dry out. Bake 20 to 30 minutes at 350 degrees. Add cut up lettuce, tomatoes, and onions to meat dish and serve.

Mable Brister

Tuna Patties

1 (6 1/2 oz.) can chunk tuna
3/4 c. cracker crumbs

1/2 c. ketchup
1 egg

Mix together well; shape into patties and fry until golden brown.

Jan Weatherley

Western Hash

1 lb. ground beef
1/2 c. chopped onion
3 1/2 c. canned tomatoes
1/2 tsp. salt
American cheese slices

1/2 c. chopped bell pepper
1 tsp. basil
1/2 c. uncooked rice
Dash pepper

Brown onion, bell pepper and beef in skillet. Drain. Add tomatoes, rice, basil, salt and pepper. Cover and simmer for 25 minutes, stirring occasionally.
Put in casserole dish and top with cheese slices. Heat until cheese is melted and serve hot. Serves 6.

Cindy Binder

Tempting Main Dish Ideas

When broiling meats or bacon on a rack, place a piece or two of dry bread in the broiler pan to soak up the dripped fat. This not only helps to eliminate smoking of the fat but reduces the chances of the fat catching fire.

Tenderizing Meat - Mechanical methods: Grinding, cubing and pounding meat breaks down the connective tissue and makes meat tender. Marinating: Soaking meat in acid mixtures such as lemon juice or vinegar tenderizes meat and adds flavor. Often herbs and spices are included in commercial marinades. Meat tenderizers: These are derivatives of natural food-tenderizing agents found in some tropical fruits (such as papaya) which soften meat tissue only while meat is cooking.

For juicier burgers, add a stiffly beaten egg white to each pound of hamburger, or make patties with one tablespoon of cottage cheese in the center.

Marbled beef, which has intermingling of fat with lean, indicates tenderness and rich flavor.

Pork chops which are light in color are corn fed.

If you rub the skin of a chicken with mayonnaise before baking, the skin will get crisp and brown.

A half teaspoon of dry mustard added to a flour mix for frying chicken adds great flavor.

The darker the flesh of a fish, the higher it is in calories.

Rule of thumb for cooking fish: Cook 10 minutes for each inch of thickness.

To keep raw fish fresh and odorless, rinse them with fresh lemon juice and water, dry thoroughly, wrap and refrigerate.

For fluffier omelets, add a pinch of cornstarch before beating.

Bacon will lie flat in the pan if you prick it thoroughly with a fork as it fries.

Tenderize tough meat by rubbing both sides with vinegar and olive oil. Let it stand two hours before cooking.

To shape meatballs, use an ice cream scoop to make uniform balls.

Meat, Poultry and Seafood

Spring House ~ Evening Shade, Arkansas

Alaskan Jerkey

Venison, cut in strips	1/2 c. worcestershire sauce
1/2 c. soy sauce	1 tbsp. onion powder
1 tbsp. garlic powder	1 tbsp. black pepper
1 tbsp. liquid smoke	1 tsp. red pepper
Tabasco sauce (about 12-16 drops)	

Marinate venison in glass container 8-12 hours. Drain & place in pan in 150 degree oven for 12 hours. You can lay meat on a cookie sheet, but drain off liquid as needed. Be sure not to fill jar too full.

Ann Horn

Baked Fish

Sprinkle salt & red pepper over fish on top of stove, heat. DO NOT BOIL!

1 lb. butter or oleo	2 tbsp. soy sauce
2 tbsp. lemon juice	

Place fish in baking dish. Pour sauce over fish; bake uncovered at 325 degrees for about 40 minutes.

Kathy Foree

Barbequed Chicken and Skillet Barbeque Sauce

3 tbsp. catsup	2 tbsp. vinegar
1 tbsp. lemon juice	2 tbsp. worcestershire
4 tbsp. water	2 tbsp. melted butter
2 tbsp. brown sugar	1 tsp. salt
1 tsp. mustard	1 tsp. chili powder
1 tsp. paprika	1/2 tsp. pepper

Brown chicken; drain. Pour sauce over chicken. Let simmer on low heat for 15 minutes.

Johnnie Whitten

Broiled Hamburger Steak

2 lbs. hamburger	Worcestershire sauce
McCormick's broiled steak season.	Dried onion flakes
4 oz. can sliced mushrooms	Salt
Pepper	Margarine

Shape hamburger into patties and put in broiling pan. Salt and pepper to taste. On each pattie, sprinkle worcestershire sauce, steak seasoning and onion flakes to your taste. Put 1/4 tsp. margarine on top of each pattie; broil for 15 minutes. Turn patties over and put seasonings on the other side. Cover with mushrooms and finish broiling, about 15 minutes. Serves 4-6.

Sandra Williams

Cajun Chicken Casserole with Cornbread Crust

2 1/2 lbs. cooked chicken, diced	1/4 c. onion minced
1/4 c. green pepper minced	1/4 c. celery diced
2 cans cream of mushroom soup	1/4 c. diced pimentos

Combine chicken and other ingredients in large bowl. Stir well. Pour into 9" X 14" pan, or individual casserole dishes.

1/2 lb. (8 oz.) cornbread mix commercial
8 oz. chicken stock, double strength   1/4 c. melted butter

Combine in large bowl. Stir well. Sprinkle over casserole(s). Bake in oven at 350 degrees until crust is golden and casserole is bubbly, about 15-20 minutes. Yield: 10 servings.
10 oz. filling, plus 2 oz. crust

Kathy Haley

Chicken and Macaroni

1 c. uncooked macaroni	1 1/2 c. chicken, diced
1 c. tomatoes	1/2 c. onion
1/4 c. milk	Salt and pepper to taste

Cook macaroni as directed on package. Cook chicken; remove from broth; debone and dice. Return chicken, tomatoes, onion, and macaroni to broth. Bring to boil; mix well and add salt and pepper. Pour in 2 qt. baking dish and add milk. Bake in oven at 350 degrees for 35 or 40 minutes.

Flava Carter

Chicken & Rice Casserole

8 boneless chicken breasts	1 can mushroom soup
1 can celery soup	2 c. milk
Salt & pepper to taste	1 1/2 c. uncooked rice

Butter bottom and sides of a 13x9x2 baking pan. Arrange chicken in bottom of pan. In large bowl mix soups and milk. Salt and pepper; add rice; mix well. Pour mixture over chicken. Cover pan. Bake for 45 minutes at 350 degrees. Uncover and bake another 15 minutes.

Wanda Kunkel

Chicken & Broccoli

3/4 lb. boned, skinned breast of chicken, slivered

2 tsp. oil	1 pkg. chopped broccoli
1 c. water	1 tbsp. dry cooking sherry
1 can cream of chicken soup	1 1/2 c. minute rice
2 slices American cheese	1 tbsp. grated Parmesan cheese

Brown chicken in the oil until cooked, about 5 minutes. Add the broccoli, water, sherry, and soup and bring to boil. Stir in rice, cut cheese into 1/4 pieces, place on top of mixture, cover, remove from heat. Let stand 5 minutes, stir, sprinkle Parmesan cheese on top and serve. Makes about 4 servings.

Donna S. Taylor

30

Chicken & Rice Dinner

2 c. uncooked rice
1 can cream of mushroom soup
1/2 stick butter
2 1/2 c. milk
1 whole chicken, cut in pieces or 8 chicken breasts
1 can chopped mushrooms
2 sm. chopped onions
2 pkg. onion soup mix

Mix rice, milk, soup, onions, mushrooms and 1 pkg. onion soup mix; mix together in lg. bowl. Pour into 9x10" dish or pan with 1/2 stick butter, cubed in bottom. Place chicken, skin side up on top of rice mixture. Sprinkle 1 pkg. onion soup mix on top. Cover with foil. Bake at 350 degrees for 45 minutes. Uncover and bake at 450 degrees for 15 minutes or until brown on top. Serves 8.

Geraldine Kunkel

Chicken & Rice with Cheese

1 onion, chopped
3 c. chicken broth
1 1/2 c. cut up, cooked chicken
1/2 tsp. salt
1 tbsp. butter or margarine
1 c. uncooked rice
1/2 c. cut up cheese

Chop onion and lightly saute' in butter. Add both and salt, heat to boiling then add rice. Stir; then cover over low heat for 20 minutes. Add chicken and cheese to rice and cook slowly until cheese is melted. Then if you want, stir in parsley for color.

Debbie Stewart

Chicken & Stuffing Casserole

1 (10 3/4 oz.) can cream of mushroom soup
1 (10 3/4 oz.) can cream of celery soup
1/2 c. milk 6 c. cooked chicken, chopped
1 (6 oz.) pkg. chicken flavored stuffing mix

Combine soups and milk in a large bowl; mix well and stir in chicken. Spoon into a 12x8x2 baking dish. Prepare stuffing mix according to package directions. Spoon evenly over chicken mixture. Cover and bake at 350 degrees for 20 minutes. Remove, cover and bake an additional 15 minutes. Serves 8.

Joyce Hancock

Chicken Casserole

Boil, salt, and de-bone whole fryer.
Mix: 1 can cream of chicken soup
1 can Rotel tomatoes
1 can mushrooms, optional
1 can cream of mushroom soup
1/2-3/4 can water
Add chicken and mix well.

Line oblong pan with Doritos or Tortilla chips. Top with cheese. Pour chicken soup mixture over this. Add more cheese and chips. Bake at 350 degrees for 20-30 minutes.

Bernell Cole

Chicken Coronet

6 chicken breasts
2 cans of cream of chicken soup

2 pkg. frozen broccoli
1/2 c. mayonnaise (not miracle whip)

1/2 tsp. curry powder
Grated lemon peel and 1 Tbsp. juice

1/2 c. grated cheddar cheese

Boil chicken for 35 minutes. Cool and bone, leaving chicken in large pieces. Thaw broccoli and put in bottom of rather flat casserole dish. Top with chicken. Stir together soup, mayonnaise, curry and lemon. Pour over chicken and sprinkle with cheese. Bake uncovered at 350 degrees for 30 to 45 minutes. Serve over plain or yellow rice with a fruit salad.

Lena Herrington

Chicken Enchiladas

1 pkg. flour tortillas
Monterey Jack cheese (grated)
1 sm. can of green chilies

5 or 6 boiled chicken breasts
2 cans cream of chicken soup

Open tortilla, spread with soup and green chili mixture, add pieces of chicken and cheese. Roll up. Lay in a greased dish that has soup spread in bottom. Pour remaining soup on top. Sprinkle with cheese. Bake at 350 degrees for 25 minutes.

Deanna Strobbe

Chicken Pie

1 whole chicken (boiled and deboned and chopped)
4 tbsp. butter or margarine
1 c. milk
1/8 tsp. cream of tartar
2/3 c. milk

3 tbsp. flour
2 c. self-rising flour
1/2 c. shortening

Boil chicken with enough water to cover; season with a dash of salt and pepper. Cool; debone; place chopped chicken in 9x13 casserole dish. In sauce pan melt butter and add flour. Stir to make paste. Add 3 cups chicken broth and 1 cup milk. Cook until you have a medium sauce. Pour over chicken in casserole dish. Mix 2 cups flour, cream of tartar, and butter and 2/3 cup milk to make soft buscuit dough. Roll out and cut with doughnut cutter leaving hole in center. Place these doughnut biscuits on top of chicken and sauce. Bake at 350 degrees for 25 to 30 minutes or until golden brown.

Leta Engle

Chicken Spaghetti

1 chicken boiled and deboned	1 lb. spaghetti
1 lb. velveeta cheese	1 can cream of mushroom soup
1 can cream of chicken soup	1 can Rotel tomatoes
1/2 chopped onion	1/2 c. chopped green pepper
1/2 c. chopped celery	1 sm. jar pimento

Cook chicken and keep broth; cook spaghetti in broth. Saute' onions, pepper, and celery. Mix soups, Rotel tomatoes, and pimento; add cheese; stir and heat until cheese melts. Add chicken and pour over spaghetti and heat all ingredients together.

Donna S. Taylor

Chicken In A Pot

1-3 lb. chicken, cut up	2 carrots sliced
2 onions sliced	2 tsp. salt
2 celery stalks with leaves, cut in 1 inch pieces	
1/2 tsp. black pepper	1/2 c. water or broth
1/2 tsp. basil	

Put carrots, onions and celery in bottom of crock pot. Add chicken pieces. Top with salt, pepper and liquid. Sprinkle basil over top. Cover and cook until done. Low: 7 to 10 hours. (High: 2 1/2 to 3 1/2 hours). Remove chicken and vegetables with spatula.

Cora Lou Davis

Dijon Chicken

Fillet chicken breasts	1/4 c. brown sugar
6 tbsp. grey poupon mustard	1 tbsp. vegetable oil

Line pan with foil and mix ingredients. Dip chicken in sauce. Bake on high at 375 degrees for 30 minutes; basting occasionally.

Ralphaine Copeland

Dorito Chicken Casserole

1 bag Nacho Chips	1 chicken, boiled and deboned
1 can cream of mushroom soup	1 can cream of chicken soup
1 sm. onion, diced	American cheese

Mix all ingredients other than chips. Layer chips and mixture in oblong casserole dish. Top with cheese. Heat in oven until cheese melts.

Mert Howard

French Style Beef Roast

3 lb. beef boneless chuck or rolled rump roast

1 tsp. salt	1 tsp. dried thyme leaves
1 bay leaf	1 lg. clove garlic, cut into fourths
6 whole cloves	5 peppercorns
4 c. water	
4 med. carrots, cut in halves	2 med. onions, cut into fourths
2 med. turnips, cut into fourths	
2 med. stalks celery cut into 1-inch pieces	

Place beef, salt, bay leaf, garlic, cloves and peppercorns in 4 qt. Dutch oven; add water. Heat to boiling; reduce heat. Cover and simmer 2 1/2 hours. Add remaining ingredients. Cover and simmer until beef and vegetables are tender, about 30 minutes. Remove beef; cut into 1/4 inch slices. Serve vegetables with beef. Strain broth; serve with beef and vegetables. Makes 8 servings; 300 calories per serving.

Luauana Underwood

Garden Chicken

1 tbsp. oil	1 1/2 lbs. chicken parts
1 med. potato, sliced	2/3 c. sliced carrots
1/2 c. green beans	2 envelopes Lipton cream of chicken
2/3 c. water	flavor or cream of mushroom cup-a-soup

In medium skillet, heat oil and brown chicken; drain. Add vegetables and soup mix blended with water. Simmer and cover 45 minutes or until tender. Serves two.

Flava Carter

Meatloaf Burgers

1 lb. hamburger meat	1 sm. onion, diced
1/2 c. oats or crushed crackers	1 egg
1/4 c. steak sauce	1 tsp. salt
1/4 c. milk	

Mix all ingredients together. Form into patties. Fry in a small amount of shortening.

Judy Wolfe

Mexican Casserole

2 or 3 c. boiled chicken	6 1/4 oz. Dorito chips
1 (10 oz.) chicken broth	1 med. onion, chopped
1 bell pepper, chopped	1 can Rotel tomatoes
1 can cream of mushroom soup	1 can cream of celery soup
8 oz. cheddar cheese, grated	

In 9x13 butter dish, layer crushed chips, chicken, chicken broth, onion and pepper. Mix other ingredients (except cheese). Pour over casserole, top with grated cheese. Bake uncovered at 350 degrees for 30-40 minutes.

Matthew Brown

Mexican Chicken

Boil whole chicken and bone
1 tsp. chili powder
1 1/2 c. chicken soup
1 can Rotel green chilies & tomatoes
1/4 lg. onion

1 pkg. tortilla chips
1 can cream of celery soup
6 oz. grated cheddar cheese

1 bell pepper

Cook onion and pepper in butter till tender; combine with broth, chicken and soups - heat. Layer as follows: chips, chicken, soup, top with Rotel and cheese. Bake at 350 degrees for 30 minutes or cheese bubbles.

Sharon Qualls

Oriental Chicken

2 c. cooked chicken
1 sm. can mushrooms
1 c. chopped celery
1 sm. can chow mein noodles

3/4 c. mayonnaise
1 can cream of chicken soup
1/2 c. chopped onion
1/2 c. slivered almonds

Mix. Bake in buttered dish at 350 degrees for 30 minutes. Serves 4-6.

Deanna Strobbe

Shake and Bake Chicken

2 c. dry bread crumbs
2 tbsp. paprika
1/4 c. shortening
2 tsp. onion powder
1 tsp. of red pepper

1/4 c. of flour
4 tsp. salt
2 tsp. sugar
2 tsp. ground oregano
1 tsp. garlic powder

Mix all together until crumbly. Store in covered container. Makes about 3 cups. Bake in 350 degree oven for about 1 1/2 hours.

Etheleen Johns

Smothered Steak

2 lbs. round steak
2 cans cream of chicken soup

salt and pepper, to taste

Cut up steak into serving size pieces; salt and pepper. Place on double duty aluminum paper. Add soup, straight from cans. Add no water! Wrap again in foil. Seal edges well to make sure it is tightly sealed and will not leak out. Bake at 325 degrees for 2 1/2 hours.

Becky James

Steak & Brown Gravy

1 charcoal or round steak cut into small cubes
2 pkgs. brown gravy mix   1/2 can tomato sauce
Salt & pepper to taste

Fry cubes in a small amount of shortening. Drain off excess grease. Add salt and pepper. Mix the gravy, according to directions. (It's better to be mixed in a shaker jar). Pour onto cooked steak. Let thicken and add 1/2 can tomato sauce. Simmer about 10 minutes. Serve over rice or mashed potatoes.

Judy Wolfe

Thanksgiving Dinner

1 car (or some mode of transportation)
1 tank of gas (depends on distance to drive)
1 pocketful of money (for gas....depends on ingredient #2)
1 empty stomach (or 2 if you bring your spouse....yes, and more if you bring the children)
1 safe trip to your mother's house

Depending on how far you have to drive (pack clothes for an overnight trip) get up early on Thanksgiving day and go to your mother's house. If travelling a long distance use plenty of ingredients 2 and 3. Upon arriving at your destination, prepare your nostrils for some luscious, mouth-watering smells. Help your mother prepare a wonderful dinner (or stay out of the way). Sit down at the table, say grace, and enjoy, enjoy, enjoy. To help make the dinner more enjoyable (especially to your mother) wash the dishes.

Janet Schwartz

36

Breads and Rolls

Spring House ~ Evening Shade, Arkansas

African Fritters

1 1/4 c. pancake or waffle mix
1 egg
1/2 tsp. vanilla
4 or 5 medium sized ripe bananas, peeled
1/3 c. sugar

1 c. milk
1 tsp. vegetable oil

1/2 tsp. cinnamon

Combine pancake mix, milk, egg, oil and vanilla in medium bowl. Mix well. Cut bananas into 1 inch pieces, coat in batter, and drain slightly. Fry about 6 at a time in 1 inch of hot oil for 1 or 2 minutes, turning frequently until brown. Drain on paper towels. Roll in cinnamon and sugar.

JoAnn Flynn

Artie Buns

Mix 1 pkg. yeast with warm water until it is creamy. Add 1 pint warm water, 4 tablespoons shortening, 1 tablespoon salt and 6 tablespoons of sugar. Mix well; work in flour to make real stiff. Let rise 1 hour make out into loafs or rolls and let rise until double in size. Grease top and then let rise.
Bake in 375 degree oven.

Anna Lee Little

Banana Hot Cakes

2 eggs
1 tsp. soda
1 Tbsp. sugar
1 tsp. banana extract
1/4 c. melted butter
1 c. thin sliced bananas (I mash them)

2 c. buttermilk
1 tsp. salt
2 tsp. baking powder
2 c. sifted flour

Beat eggs until light and fluffy. Blend in buttermilk, soda, salt, sugar, baking powder and banana extract. Beat until smooth. Gradually blend in flour and mix to smooth batter. Fold in melted butter and banana slices. Cook on lightly oiled griddle. Serve immediately with favorite syrup and whipped butter or banana flavored whipped cream (makes 10-12 cakes).

Elizabeth Walker

Best Ever Muffins

1 3/4 c. sifted flour
2 1/2 tsp. baking powder
1 well beaten egg
1/2 c. oil

2 Tbsp. sugar
3/4 tsp. salt
3/4 c. milk

Sift dry ingredients into mixing bowl. Make a well in the center. Combine egg, milk, and salad oil. Add all at once to dry ingredients. Stir quickly only until dry ingredients are moist. Fill greased muffin pans 2/3 full. Bake at 400 degrees about 25 minutes. Makes 12 muffins.

Cheryl Watkins

37

Biscuits

2 c. of plain flour
1/4 tsp. salt
1/2 c. of crisco

4 1/2 tsp. of baking powder
1/4 tsp. sugar
1 c. of milk

Sift flour, baking powder, salt and sugar together in medium size bowl. Cut crisco into dry ingredients; stir milk into mixture. Drop onto greased sheet or roll out on flour board and place on ungreased sheet. Bake at 425 for 15-20 minutes.

Virginia Qualls

Coffeecake

1/4 c. salad oil
1/2 c. milk
1/4 c. sugar
1/2 tsp. salt

1 beaten egg
1 1/2 c. flour
2 tsp. baking powder
Topping, below

Combine salad oil, egg, and milk. Sift together dry ingredients; add to milk mixture; mix well. Pour into greased 9x9x2" pan.

Topping: Combine 1/4 c. brown sugar, 1 Tbsp. flour, 1 tsp. cinnamon, 1 Tbsp. melted butter, and 1/2 c. broken nuts; sprinkle over batter. Bake in moderate oven, 375 degrees, for about 25 minutes.

Cheryl Watkins

Cornbread

1 c. flour
4 tsp. baking powder
1 c. corn meal
1 c. milk

1/4 c. sugar
3/4 tsp. salt
2 eggs
1/4 c. salad oil

Mix all ingredients together and bake at 425 degrees for 20-25 minutes.

Elizabeth Walker

Cranberry Bread

2 c. sifted flour
1 c. sugar
1 1/2 c. cranberries, chopped
1/2 tsp. salt
1 egg, beaten
2 Tbsp. hot water

1 1/2 tsp. baking powder
1/2 c. chopped nuts
2 Tbsp. melted shortening or oil
1/2 tsp. soda
1/2 c. orange juice

Sift dry ingredients; add shortening and egg. Then add nuts and cranberries; last add hot water. Bake in greased loaf pan at 350 degrees for 1 hour and 10 minutes.

Mary Wilson

Doughnuts

3 Tbsp. shortening	3/4 c. sugar
2 eggs	1/4 c. milk
2 1/2 c. flour	3 tsp. baking powder
1 tsp. salt	1 c. mashed potatoes

Cream shortening and sugar. Add eggs and milk. Stir in mashed potatoes. Sift dry ingredients together and add to creamed mixture. Roll out dough to 1/2 inch thickness. Cut with doughnut cutter. Fry in deep fat at 375 degrees for 2-4 minutes.

Helen Cushman

Easy Biscuits

1 c. milk	1/3 c. vegetable oil
2 c. W.R. Self-rising flour	

Mix milk and oil in mixing bowl. Add flour and mix to make soft dough. Turn out on floured board or pastry sheet. Knead lightly and roll out to about 1/2 inch. Cut with floured biscuit cutter. Oil 9 inch cake pan with 2 or 3 tablespoons vegetable oil. Place biscuits in pan and oil tops. Bake in 500 degree oven for 10 to 15 minutes or until golden brown. Makes 8 biscuits.

Laurie Davis

Easy Refrigerator Rolls

1 pkg. dry yeast	2 c. warm water (105-115 degrees)
3/4 c. butter or margarine, melted	1/4 c. sugar
1 egg beaten	4 c. self rising flour

Dissolve yeast in water, let stand 5 minutes. Combine butter and sugar in a large bowl stirring well. Add yeast mixture and egg, stirring until blended. Gradually stir in flour. (Mixture will resemble batter rather than dough). Cover tightly and refrigerate at least 8 hours or up to 3 days before using. Spoon dough into greased muffins pan - 2/3 full. Cover and let rise 30 minutes in a warm place (85 degrees). Bake at 350 degrees for 20 minutes or until golden brown.

Joyce Hancock

Frozen French Toast

2 eggs	1 c. milk
1 Tbsp. sugar	1/4 tsp. salt
12 slices bread	

In bowl, beat together eggs, milk, sugar and salt. Dip bread in egg mixture to coat. Brown on both sides on greased griddle or in skillet. Place on baking sheet and freeze. When firm, wrap in foil, using 2 sices for each package with wax paper between slices. Return to freezer immediately. To serve, place bread slice in toaster - toast. Spread with oleo and warmed syrup.

Maple Flavored Syrup - On Next Page

Maple Flavored Syrup

1 c. light corn syrup
1/2 c. water
1/4 tsp. maple flavoring

1/2 c. brown sugar
1 Tbsp. oleo or butter

In saucepan, mix corn syrup, brown sugar and water; cook and stir until sugar is dissolved. Reduce heat and simmer five minutes. Add oleo and flavoring. Makes 1 2/3 cups syrup.

Jane Graddy

Hush Puppies

2 c. cornmeal mix
1 lg. onion, finely chopped
Milk

2 eggs
1 Tbsp. sugar

Mix all ingredients; add just enough milk to make a stiff batter. Have corn oil in fry daddy hot. Roll mixture into balls and fry until golden brown. Watch carefully that it doesn't take but a few minutes to fry.

Becky James

Mexican Corn Bread

1 c. corn meal
1 c. yellow cream style corn
1 c. sour milk
2 eggs
1 onion

1/2 tsp. salt
1/2 c. vegetable oil
1/2 tsp. soda
1/3 chopped pepper
1 c. grated cheese

Mix all ingredients using 1/2 of cheese in the batter. Pour into greased skillet. Sprinkle other 1/2 of cheese over batter. Bake at 375 degrees until golden brown.

Linda Campbell

Mexican Corn Bread

1 1/2 lb. ground beef
1 med. bell pepper chopped
1/2 tsp. red pepper
3/4 c. milk
4 slices bacon, cooked & crumbled
1 1/2 c. grated cheese

1 med. onion chopped
1 1/2 c. corn meal mix
2 eggs
1 16 oz. can cream style corn
1/3 c. bacon drippings
1 can Rotel tomatoes

Brown ground beef; pour off fat, if any. Add onion and green pepper and simmer until vegetables are tender. Set aside.

Mix corn meal mix, red pepper, eggs, milk and cream corn. Add bacon drippings. Pour half of cornbread mixture into a greased 9x13 baking pan. Layer ground beef, crumbled bacon, cheese and Rotel tomatoes. Pour rest of cornbread mixture over all. Bake at 400 degrees for 35-45 minutes.

Joyce Hancock

40

Never Fail Yeast Rolls

2 pkgs. Active Dry Yeast (not quick rise)
2 c. warm water   1 large egg, lightly beaten
1/4 to 1/2 c. sugar (depending on taste)
Flour to consistency (4-6 cups, approx.)

In large bowl, mix first 4 ingredients until yeast is dissolved. Let set for 10 minutes. Add flour a little bit at a time, until dough just lightly sticks to fingers when kneading. Cover, set in warm area; let rise to double size. Turn out onto floured board and knead 5 times. Pinch off roll size pieces and place in 9"x 13" pan that is greased. Cover and let rise again, to double size. Bake at 350 degrees until tops are golden brown. Butter tops and serve. Makes 30-40 rolls.

Steve Burkhart

Nut Bread

3 c. all purpose flour   1 c. sugar
4 tsp. baking powder   1 tsp. salt
1 beaten egg   1 1/2 c. milk
1/4 c. cooking oil   3/4 c. chopped walnuts

Stir thoroughly the first 4 ingredients. Combine egg, milk, and oil; add to dry ingredients, beating well. Stir in nuts. Turn into greased 8 1/2 x 4 1/2 x 2 1/2" loaf pan. Bake at 350 degrees about 70 minutes. Remove from pan; cool on rack. Makes 1 loaf.

Rena Bowser

Pecan Rolls

2 c. sugar   1/2 c. light corn syrup
1/2 c. water   1 large egg white
1 tsp. vanilla   3 c. pecans, coursely chopped

In 2qt. pan over medium heat stir sugar, corn syrup and water until sugar dissolves and mixture boils with out stirring; boil gently until candy reaches 250. Just before syrup reaches 250 degrees in a small bowl beat egg white and vanilla until soft peaks form. Beating constantly, slowly pour hot syrup mixture over egg whites. Continue beating for about 10 to 12 minutes, or until stiff peak forms. Divide into sixths; shape into 4x1 inch rolls. Wrap in saran wrap. Refrigerate at least 4 hours, or until cold and firm. A day or two if you like. When ready to coat rolls spread pecans on a cookie sheet. Prepare carmel coating and remove from heat. When mixture stops boiling lower rolls into coating 1 at a time. Coat completely and roll in pecans. Cool and whip.

Caramel Coating

In 2qt. pan over low heat, stirring constantly, mix and bring to a boil:
One 14oz. can sweetened condensed milk
1 c. sugar   1/2 c. light corn syrup   1/3 tsp. salt

Continue cooking over low heat, stirring constantly, until candy reaches 234 degrees, about 1 hour. Use as directed in Pecan Rolls.

Maleta Engle

Poritzal

1 c. flour
1/2 c. raisins
Milk
1/2 c. sugar
3 tsp. baking powder

Mix dry ingredients and raisins. Add milk until consistency of batter is about the same as hush puppies. Make into balls. Deep fry in cooking oil at about 300 to 350 degrees until golden brown or until they are floating. Makes 6. Optional: Roll in powdered sugar when done.

Luauana Underwood

Pumpkin Bread

1 tsp. baking powder
1 can (16 ozs.) pumpkin
2/3 c. water
4 eggs
2 tsp. salt
1 tsp. pumpkin pie spice
1 c. salad oil
2 tsp. baking soda
3 c. sugar
3 1/2 c. sifted flour
1 tsp. cinnamon

Soak one cup raisins in water - drain and add last by hand. Cream sugar and oil; add eggs and pumpkin, mix well and add dry ingredients. Makes one loaf pan and two 1 lb. coffee cans full. Fill either loaf pans or cans half full of mixture. Cook at 350 degrees. Cool on rack. Freezes well.

Mary King

Raised Doughnuts

2 pkgs. yeast
(mix and set aside)
(Mix) 1/2 c. sugar
1/2 c. shortening
1 c. warm water

2 tsp. salt

(Add) 1 c. scalded milk, cool; add 2 eggs (well beaten)
(Add) yeast and water mixture   (Add) 6 c. sifted flour.

Knead on floured board until smooth but not real stiff. Place in large oiled bowl and let rise until doubled in bulk. Place on floured board and roll out to 1/2 inch thick. Cut with doughnut cutter. Let rise again for about 30 minutes. Fry in 1 inch hot oil then dip in glaze.

Doughnut Glaze

3 c. sugar
1/2 tsp. vanilla
3/4 c. of milk
1/2 stick margarine

Mix all ingredients and cook in saucepan over medium heat until it forms a soft ball in cold water. Dip doughnuts as soon as they are fried.

Cora Lou Davis

Refrigerator Rolls

1 pkg. yeast	1 1/2 c. warm water
1 tsp. sugar	1/2 c. shortening
1/2 c. sugar	2 tsp. salt
1 egg	4 1/2 c. bread flour
	(omit part of salt if self-rising flour is used)

Soften yeast in warm water with 1 tsp. of sugar added. Mix 1 shortening and 1/2 cup sugar and salt. Cream together. Add egg and beat well. Add yeast mixture and half the flour. Mix well. Add remaining flour and let stand 10 minutes. Knead lightly. Place in greased bowl and cover and store in regrigerator.

Use rolls as needed. Pinch off dough to desired size and let rise until double in size. Bake at 425 for 15 to 20 minutes.

Unused portion of dough may be returned to refrigerator until needed. Keep for a week to 10 days.

Bobby Smith

Sour Dough Biscuits

1 pkg. yeast	1 c. warm water
2 c. buttermilk	3/4 c. corn oil
6 or more c. flour	1/4 c. sugar
4 tsp. baking powder	2 tsp. salt
1/4 tsp. soda	

Dissolve yeast in warm water. Add sugar, buttermilk and oil. Sift together flour, salt, baking powder and soda. Add to liquid. Place dough in covered bowl and refrigerate overnight. Pinch off amount wanted for meal. Bake at 450 degrees for 10-15 minutes or until brown. No need to let rise before baking. Keep remaining dough in the refrigerator.

Geraldine Kunkel

Sweet Potato Biscuits

2 c. mashed (boiled) sweet potatoes
1 c. molasses   1/2 c. buttermilk
1 tsp. soda   1/2 c. shortening
Flour (approx. 3 cups self-rising)

Work in enough self-rising flour to handle. If plain flour is used, add 1/2 tsp. salt and 1 tsp. baking powder. Roll and cut out like ordinary biscuits.
Bake at 350 degrees. Serve hot with butter.

David Paul

Vinegar Pastry

Into mixing bowl, sift together: 3 c. flour (sifted), 1 Tbsp. sugar, 3/4 tsp. salt, 1/2 tsp. baking powder. Cut in 1 1/4 c. shortening until it resembles small peas. Combine 1 egg, 5 Tbsp. water and 1 Tbsp. vinegar. Sprinkle 4 Tbsp. of this over mix and then mix lightly with a fork. Add 4 more Tbsp. of egg mixture. Continue mixing until pastry holds together. Press into a ball. Wrap in plastic or waxed paper and chill 15 minutes. Divide in half and roll between 2 pieces of clear plastic wrap.

Jane Graddy

Whole Wheat Muffins

Cream 4 Tbsp. of butter with 4 Tbsp. of sugar and add 2 well beaten eggs. Add one cup of milk and 1 1/2 cup of whole wheat flour, 2 tsp. of baking powder and 1/2 tsp. salt. Mix then pour into greased muffin tin pan and bake at 400 degrees until brown.

Hatty Gentry

Zucchini Bread

3 eggs beaten
2 c. grated zucchini
2 c. sugar

1 c. cooking oil
3 tsp. vanilla
3 tsp. cinnamon

Mix above ingredients. Add:

1 tsp. baking soda
1/2 tsp. baking powder
3 c. flour

1/2 tsp. salt
1/2 c. chopped nuts

Bake at 350 degrees for about 1 hour. Makes 2 loaves.

Luauana Underwood

Pies, Pastry and Desserts

Spring House ~ Evening Shade, Arkansas

Apple Crisp

1 can apple pie filing
3/4 c. quick oatmeal
1/2 c. butter

1 c. brown sugar
1 tbsp. cinnamon
3/4 c. flour

Spread apple pie filling in bottom of pan. Combine other ingredients. Mix until crumbly. Put over apples. Bake at 350 degrees 45 to 50 minutes or until top is golden brown. (Good with cherry pie filling also).

Debbie Stewart

Apple Pie and Easy Crust

1 1/4 c. flour
1 stick butter or oleo
4 c. grated apples (1 c. sugar for sour apples)
1/4 tsp. pumpkin pie spice
3 or 4 tbsp. water

1/2 c. sugar
1/2 tsp. cinnamon

2 tbsp. cornstarch
10 inch pie plate

Mix flour, sugar, cinnamon, and butter. Crumble 2/3 of this mixture in bottom of pie plate and press down. Mix apples, sugar (for sour apples), spice, cornstarch, and water. Pour into crust and sprinkle the rest of crust mixture over top of apples. Bake at 350 degrees for about 35 to 40 minutes or until golden brown. NOTE: adjust sugar for tartness of apples.

Linda Campbell

Banana Pudding

1 lg. Cool Whip
1 can Eagle Brand milk
1 1/2 c. milk

1 lg. vanilla instant pudding
Vanilla wafers
Bananas

Mix pudding and milk together. Add Eagle Brand, mix well; fold in Cool Whip. Layer pudding mixture bananas and vanilla wafers. Let set for 1 to 1 1/2 hours before serving.

Ann Horn

Brownie Pudding

1 c. self rising flour
1/2 c. unsweetened cocoa, divided
2 tbsp. vanilla
1/2 c. firmly packed brown sugar
1 T. butter
Peppermint, coffee, or vanilla ice cream

1/2 c. granulated sugar
1/2 c. milk
1/2 c. semi sweet chocolate chips
1 3/4 c. boiling water

Preheat oven to 350 degrees. Combine flour, granulated sugar, and 1/4 cup cocoa in bowl. Stir in milk, butter, and vanilla until smooth. Stir in chocolate chips. Spread in ungreased shallow 1 1/2 qt. casserole dish. Sprinkle brown sugar and 1/4 cup cocoa on top. Place in oven, pour boiling water over top. Bake 35 minutes. Cool 10 minutes before serving. Serve with ice cream. Serves 6.

Joyce Hancock

Cherry Cheese Pie

1-9 oz. graham cracker crust
1-14 oz. can Eagle Brand milk
1 tsp. vanilla
1-8oz. pkg. cream cheese
1/3 c. lemon juice
1-21oz. can cherry pie filling

In large mixer bowl beat cheese until smooth. Gradually beat in Eagle Brand milk; stir in lemon juice and vanilla. Pour into crust. Refrigerate until set, add cherry pie filling. Keep refrigerated.

Maleta Engle

Chess Pie

1/2 c. butter or margarine
1 tbsp. all-purpose flour
5 well-beaten eggs
1 tsp. vanilla
1 unbaked Rich Pastry Shell
2 c. sugar
1 tbsp. yellow cornmeal
1 c. milk
2 tbsp. lemon juice

Cream butter and sugar; beat in flour and cornmeal. Add eggs, milk, vanilla, and lemon juice; beat well. Pour into pastry shell. Bake in moderate oven (350 degrees) 55 to 60 minutes, or till knife comes out clean.

Rich Pastry Shell: Sift together 1 cup sifted all-purpose flour, 1/4 tsp. salt, and 1/4 tsp. baking powder. Cut in 6 tbsp. butter or margarine till the size of small peas. Gradually add 3 to 4 tbsp. milk, mixing till dough can be formed into a ball. Roll out and fit into 9-inch pie plate (have edges crimped high because amount of filling is generous).

Hattie Gentry

Chocolate Oatmeal Pie

2 eggs
1 c. sugar
1/4 tsp. salt
2 tbsp. cocoa
1/2 c. margarine (melted)
2/3 c. uncooked oats
1 tsp. vanilla
1 unbaked 8" pie shell

Combine first seven ingredients in order listed. Blend well. Pour into shell and bake at 300 degrees for 45 minutes. Cool.

Virginia Qualls

Chocolate Pudding
Stove Top or Microwave

1 c. sugar
1/4 tsp. salt
2 c. milk
2 tbsp. butter - slightly melted
1/3 c. all-purpose flour
4 tbsp. cocoa
3 egg yolks - slightly beaten
1 tsp. vanilla

Combine sugar, flour, salt, and cocoa. Blend well, then add milk. Cook slowly and stir until hot (2 min. in microwave). Stir a small amount of hot mixture into egg yolks. Stir into hot mixture immediately. Cook, stirring constantly for 10 min. or until thickened. Add butter and vanilla. (6 min. in microwave and stir every 2 min.)

Tamra Binder

Chocolate Truffle Pie

1 envelope Knox Unflavored Gelatine
1/3 c. cold orange juice   1 tbsp. instant coffee
1 pkg. (6 oz.) semi-sweet chocolate chips
1 tsp. vanilla extract   2 eggs
1/4 c. sugar
1 1/2 c. heavy or whipping cream, whipped
8 or 9-inch chocolate crumb crust

In medium saucepan, sprinkle gelatine over cold orange juice; let stand 1 minute. Stir over low heat until gelatine is dissolved. Add instant coffee and chocolate and heat, stirring constantly, until chocolate is thoroughly melted. Remove from heat and stir in vanilla; let stand 10 minutes or until lukewarm. Meanwhile, in large bowl, with electric mixer at high speed, beat eggs with sugar 5 minutes or until thickened. Gradually add lukewarm gelatine mixture and beat until just thoroughly blended. Fold in whipped cream. Turn into prepared crust; chill until firm. Garnish, if desired, with whipped cream and chocolate shavings. Makes 8 servings.
* Substitution: Use 2 cups frozen whipped topping, thawed.

Holly Arnold

Coconut Cream Pie

3/4 c. coconut   1/4 c. sugar
1/2 c. cake mix (yellow)   3 egg yolks
1 1/2 c. milk   1/4 stick butter

Mix sugar, cake mix and egg yolks. Blend in enough milk to mix well. Add remaining milk; cook until thick. Add butter, then coconut and pour into baked crust.

Anna Lee Little

Cream Cheese Pineapple Pie

1/3 c. sugar   1 tbsp. cornstarch
1 can (8 oz.) crushed pineapple with juice
Cream cheese layer:
1 pkg. (8 oz.) cream cheese softened to room temp.
1/2 c. sugar   1 tsp. salt
2 eggs   1/2 c. milk
1/2 tsp. vanilla   1 9-inch unbaked pie crust
1/4 c. chopped pecans

Combine sugar, cornstarch, and pineapple plus juice in a small saucepan. Cook over medium heat, stirring constantly until mixture is thick and clear. Cool, set aside. Blend in cream cheese, sugar, and salt in mixer bowls. Add eggs, one at a time beating 2 minutes after each addition. Blend in milk and vanilla. If mixture loks lightly curdled, don't worry, it bakes out. Spread cooled pineapple layer over bottoms of pie crust. Pour cream cheese mixture over pineapple, sprinkle with pecans. Bake at 400 degrees for 10 minutes. Reduce heat to 325 and bake for 50 minutes.

Bernice Haley

Eclairs

2 pkgs. french vanilla instant pudding mix
3 c. milk   Small carton cool whip

Mix pudding mix and milk; then beat in the cool whip. Line 9 x 13 pan with graham crackers. Pour a layer of pudding mix over cracker. Add another layer of graham crackers and pudding mix; end with graham crackers.

Icing

6 tbsp. coca-cola   1 stick oleo
3 tbsp. cocoa

Bring this to a boil. Take off stove and add 1 box powdered sugar; mix with mixer. Let cake set in the refrigerator at least 1 hour before you put icing on cake.

Connie Boyle

French Coconut Pie

1 stick melted butter   3 whole eggs, beaten
1 tbsp. vinegar   1 1/2 c. sugar
1 can flake coconut   1 tsp. vanilla

Combine all ingredients and pour into unbaked pastry shell. Bake at 350 degrees for 1 hour.

Tammy Bacon

Fresh Peach Pie

Crust:
1 1/2 c. flour   1 1/2 tbsp. sugar
1 tsp. salt

Mix these ingredients together well; add 1/2 cup oil and 2 tbsp. milk. Whip together with a fork before stirring into flour mixture. It will crumble. Press into pie pan and bake until golden brown at 375 degrees.

Filling:
1 c. water   1 c. sugar
1 tbsp. cornstarch

Cook until clear and add 2 tbsp. dry orange gelatin. Cool. Pour mixture over 3 or 4 sliced fresh peaches in baked shell. Top with cream or cool whip.

Laurie Davis

Jiffy Cobbler

1 stick margarine - Melt in 9 x 13 baking pan in oven.
1 qt. fruit   1 c. sugar

Bring to a boil in sauce pan.
1 c. sugar   1 c. self rising flour
1 c. milk

Mix and pour batter over melted margarine in baking pan. Pour hot fruit over batter. Bake 45 minutes in 350 degree oven.

Carrie Barnett

Jiffy Fruit Cobbler

1 c. flour	1 c. sugar
1 stick oleo	2 1/2 tsp. baking powder
3/4 c. milk	Pinch of salt, small

Melt 1 stick of oleo in pan. While oleo melts make batter of the remaining ingredients. Pour batter into melted oleo. Do not stir. Pour 3 cups of sweetened fruit (canned or freshly cooked) into batter. Do not stir. Bake at 350 degrees for 40 minutes or until done. A delicious quick dessert.

Twana Miller

Lazy Day Pie

1 qt. sweetened peaches	1/4 c. butter
3/4 c. sugar	3/4 c. self-rising flour
1/2 c. water	

Heat peaches until hot. Melt butter in 1 1/2 quart oblong pan. Mix together sugar, flour and water. pour into greased baking dish. Pour hot peaches on top. Bake at 425 degrees for 30 minutes or until crust is brown. (This recipe came from a Snow King Baking Powder Cookbook, about 50 years ago.)

Flava Carter

Meringue

3 egg whites (room temp.)	1 tsp. vanilla
1/4 tsp. cream of tarter	

Whip until very stiff; slowly add 3/4 cup sugar and beat until sugar is dissolved. Put on cream pie and bake 300 degrees for 20 minutes.

Virginia Qualls

Mock Pecan Pie

1/4 c. butter	3/4 c. sugar
2 eggs	3/4 c. white syrup
1 tsp. vanilla	1 c. coconut
3/4 c. minute oats	1 9-inch unbaked pie shell

Cream butter and sugar; mix in the eggs, corn syrup and vanilla. Stir in coconut and oats. Pour into pie shell. Bake at 350 degrees for 40-45 minutes or until golden brown.

Ann Horn

Peachy Delight

First layer:
 1 c. flour   1 tbsp. sugar
 1/2 c. margarine, softened   1/4 c. chopped pecans

Mix all ingredients for first layer and spread in 9 x 13 inch baking dish. Bake at 350 degrees for 20 minutes. Cool.

Second layer:
 1 c. sugar
 1 (8 oz.) pkg. cream cheese, softened
 1 (9 oz.) carton whipped topping   3 c. sliced fresh peaches

To prepare second layer, cream sugar and cream cheese. Fold in whipped topping. Spread mixture over crust. Top with sliced peaches.

Third layer:
 1 c. sugar   4 tbsp. cornstarch
 1 (3 oz.) pkg. peach flavored gelatin   1 1/2 cups water

To prepare third layer, combine sugar, cornstarch and water. Cook until thick. Stir in peach gelatin until thoroughly blended. Cool. Spoon glaze over peaches.

* Also good with strawberries and strawberry gelatin.

Berneice Haley

Peanut Butter Pie

 4 oz. cream cheese   1/2 c. peanut butter
 1/2 c. milk   1 c. powdered sugar
 1 (8 oz.) cool whip   1 graham cracker crust

Blend first four ingredients until smooth. Fold in cool whip. Pour into graham cracker crust.

Peanut Butter Pie

 1 baked pie shell   1 scant c. confectioners sugar
 1/2 c. peanut butter   1/4 c. cornstarch
 1/2 c. sugar   1/4 tsp. salt
 2 c. milk   3 eggs, separated
 2 tbsp. butter   1/2 tsp. vanilla

Mix powdered sugar and peanut butter together until if feels like cornmeal. Mix cornstarch, sugar, salt and egg yolks together; add milk, butter and vanilla. Cook over low heat until thickened. Pour powdered sugar and peanut mixture into pie mixture and stir just a little. Pour into baked pie shell; top with egg white beaten; bake 325 degrees until light brown about 15 minutes.

Anna Lee Little

Pecan Pie

1 unbaked pie shell
3/4 c. sugar
1 stick butter or margarine, melted
1 tsp. vanilla
1 c. dark corn syrup
3 eggs, slightly beaten
2 tbsp. flour
1 1/2 c. chopped pecans

Beat eggs. Add sugar and flour, then butter and vanilla. Add syrup and nuts. Place in pie shell. Bake for 35 to 45 minutes at 300 degrees or until done. Will be slightly puffy across top when done. Do not overcook.

Caroline Cross

Pineapple Pie

1 c. sugar
1 lg. can pineapple
2 tbsp. flour or cornstarch

Mix with pineapple; pour into crust and top with crust. Bake at 425 degrees for one hour.

Reba Taylor

Pink Lemonade Pie

1 sm can frozen pink lemonade
1 lg. box Cool Whip
1 can Eagle Brand milk
2 graham cracker crumb crusts

Combine lemonade, milk and blend; fold in Cool Whip and pour into crust. Decorate with a slice of lemon.

Leta Engle

Pudding Cake

1 pkg. (2 layer size) cake mix
1 pkg. (4 serving size) Jello instant pudding and pie filling
1 c. water
4 eggs

Combine all ingredients in large mixing bowl. Blend; then beat 2 min. Pour into a greased and flowered 10-inch Bundt or tube pan. Bake at 350 degrees for 50 minutes, or until center springs back when lightly touched. Cool 15 min. Remove from pan and finish cooling. A 13 x 9-inch pan may be used; bake 45 min.

Deltha Sharp

Pumpkin Chiffon

Crust:

1 c. flour

1 c. chopped nuts

1 stick oleo, softened

Mix all together & press in 9 x 13 pan. Bake at 350 degrees for just a few minutes (will be baked again with filling). Can use a graham cracker crust if preferred.

1st layer:

1-8 oz. pkg. cream cheese, softened

2 eggs, beaten

3/4 c. powdered sugar

1 tsp. vanilla

Combine cream cheese, eggs, sugar, & vanilla; beat until fluffy. Spread over crust. Bake at 350 degrees (325 degrees glass pan) for 20 minutes. Set aside to cool.

2nd layer:

2-3 3/4 oz. pkgs. vanilla instant pudding mix

3/4 c. milk

1 tsp. vanilla

1 can pumpkin that has had 1/4 c. powdered sugar sifted into it

1 tsp. pumpkin pie spice

1-8 oz. cool whip

Combine pudding mix & milk; beat 2 minutes at medium speed. Add pumpkin (with sugar added), vanilla, & spice; mix well. Stir in 1 cup of the cool whip, & spread mixture over cream cheese layer. Then spread remaining cool whip over pudding layer. Store in refrigerator. Yield: about 15 servings.

Debbie Hampton

Quick Chocolate Pie

1 pkg. vanilla pudding and pie filling

1 pkg. chocolate pudding and pie filling

(both packages instant)

1 c. milk

2 c. ice cream (vanilla or chocolate flavor, to your liking)

Blend all ingredients, well. Pour into prepared graham cracker crust. Chill.

Lita King

Raisin Pie

3 beaten eggs

1 c. sugar

1/2 tsp. ground cinnamon

1/2 tsp. ground nutmeg

1/2 tsp. salt

2 1/2 tbsp. lemon juice

2 tbsp. butter or margarine, melted

1 c. raisins

1/3 c. broken walnuts

1 8-inch unbaked pastry shell

Combine eggs, sugar, spices, salt, lemon juice, and butter. Stir in raisins and nuts. Pour into pastry shell. Bake in moderate oven (375 degrees) 35 to 40 minutes or until filling is set in center. Cool.

Rena Bowser

Single Pie Crust

1 1/3 c. flour   1 tsp. salt
1/3 c. wesson oil   3 tbsp. milk

Sift flour and salt. Pour oil to 1/3 of cup and add milk to 1/2 cup line. Pour into flour and mix into ball. Roll out between wax paper or heavy reynold's wrap.
For double crust, use:

2 c. flour   1/2 c. wesson oil
Add milk to 2/3 cup line.

Virginia Qualls

Strawberry Pie

Crust:

1 c. flour   1 stick oleo (melted)
1 c. nuts (I put mine in blender)

Mix these 3 ingredients and press into pie pan and bake at 400 degrees until lightly browned.
Pie Filling:

1 c. sugar   1 c. 7-Up
3 tbsp. cornstarch

Mix this and boil on high heat until very thick. Add red food coloring. Take off heat and let cool and then add 1 qt. of sliced strawberries. Pour into cooled crust and let set several hours in refrigerator before serving. Top with cool whip if desired.

Connie Boyle

Tang Pie

1 can Eagle Brand milk   1-8 oz. Cool Whip
1-8 oz. sour cream   1/2 c. Tang

Mix ingredients. Use regular crust or graham cracker crust. Makes two pies or a 9 x 13 pan.

Lita King

Vanilla Wafers

2 eggs   1/2 c. shortening
1 tsp. cream of tartar   1 1/2 to 2 c. flour
1/2 tsp. baking soda   1/2 tsp. salt
1 c. sugar   1/2 tsp. vanilla
(Leave out tartar, soda, and salt if self-rising flour is used)

Cream shortening and sugar; add eggs, vanilla and flour. Work on board and roll out 1/8 inch thick. Bake 400 degrees for 10 minutes.

Anna Lee Little

Baking Perfect Desserts

For Perfect Cookies

Cookie dough that is to be rolled is much easier to handle after it has been in a cold place 10 to 30 minutes. This keeps the dough from sticking, even though it may be soft. If not done, the soft dough may require more flour and too much flour makes cookies hard and brittle. In rolling, take out on a floured board, only as much dough as can be managed easily. Flour the rolling pin slightly and roll lightly to desired thickness. Cut shapes close together and keep all trimmings for the last. Place pans or sheets in upper third of oven. Watch cookies carefully while baking to avoid burning edges. When sprinkling sugar on cookies, try putting sugar into a salt shaker. It saves time.

For Perfect Pies and Cakes

A pie crust will be more easily made and better if all the ingredients are cool.

The lower crust should be placed in the pan so that it covers the surface smoothly. Be sure no air lurks beneath the surface, for it will push the crust out of shape in baking.

Folding the top crust over the lower crust before crimping will keep the juices in the pie.

In making custard type pies, bake at a high temperature for about ten minutes to prevent a soggy crust. Then finish baking at a low temperature.

Fill cake pans about two-thirds full and spread batter well into corners and to the sides, leaving a slight hollow in the center.

The cake is done when it shrinks from the sides of the pan or if it springs back when touched lightly with the finger.

After a cake comes from the oven, it should be placed on a rack for about five minutes. Then the sides should be loosened and the cake turned out on a rack to finish cooling.

Cakes should not be frosted until thoroughly cool.

If you want to make a pecan pie and haven't any nuts, substitute crushed cornflakes. They will rise to the top and give a delicious flavor and crunchy surface.

To prevent crust from becoming soggy with cream pie, sprinkle crust with powdered sugar.

Cut drinking straws into short lengths and insert through slits in pie crusts to prevent juices from running over in the oven and permit steam to escape.

Cakes, Cookies and Candy

Spring House ~ Evening Shade, Arkansas

Applesauce Cake

Mix together:
  2 1/2 c. unsweetened applesauce, heated
  3 1/2 tsp. soda
Cream together:
  1 c. shortening   2 c. sugar
Mix together:
  4 c. flour   1 tsp. cinnamon
  1/2 tsp. allspice   1/2 tsp. cloves
Blend all of the above dry ingredients with liquid ingredients. Add 1 c. nuts and 1 lb. raisins (2 cups).
Bake at 350 degrees for one hour.

                                              Bonnie Vandermolen

Coke Icing

  1/2 c. butter   3 Tbsp. cocoa
  6 Tbsp. coke   1 box powdered sugar
  1 c. nuts

Combine butter, cocoa and coke. Heat to boiling. Pour over sugar; after beating well, add nuts. Ice cake while still warm.

                                                  Anna Lee Little

Caramel Chocolate Cake

  1-14 oz. pkg. caramels   1/3 c. milk
  1/2 c. butter   3/4 c. chocolate chips
  1/2 c. nuts   1 German chocolate cake mix
  1 cool whip

Melt together caramels, butter and milk in double boiler. Mix cake as directed on pkg.; pour half into greased and floured 9x13 pan. Bake at 350 degrees for 15 minutes. Spread caramel mixture on top; sprinkle with chocolate chips and nuts. Pour remaining cake on top, bake 20 minutes at 250 degrees, then 10 minutes at 350 degrees. Serve either warm or cool with cool whip topping and a marachino cherry on top.

                                              Bonnie Vandermolen

Carrot Cake

  2 c. sugar   4 eggs
  2 Tbsp. vanilla   1 1/2 c. wesson oil
  2 c. flour   1 tsp. soda
  1 tsp. salt   3 tsp. cinnamon
  3 c. shredded carrots   1 c. chopped nuts

Mix sugar, eggs and vanilla together. Add oil and mix well. Add dry ingredients and mix well. Add carrots and nuts and mix until well blended.
Bake at 350 degrees for 45 minutes to 1 hour.

Frosting - Next Page

Frosting

Mix until well blended:

8 oz. pkg. cream cheese   1/2 stick margarine
1/2 box powdered sugar

Cheryl Watkins

Chocolate Sheet Cake

Mix together:

2 c. sifted flour	2 c. sugar
1 tsp. soda	2 tsp. cinnamon

Melt and bring to a boil:

1/4 c. oleo	1/2 c. shortening
4 Tbsp. cocoa	1 c. water

Add hot ingredients to dry ingredients above and mix.
Add:

1/2 c. buttermilk	2 eggs (beaten)
1 tsp. vanilla	

Bake at 400 degrees for 20 minutes in a 10x15 cookie sheet (1/2 inch sides).

Icing:

1/4 lb. oleo   6 Tbsp. milk
4 Tbsp. cocoa

Bring to a boil and add 1 lb. box powdered sugar, 1 tsp. vanilla, and 1/2 c. chopped nuts. Spread on hot cake.

Pat Ring

Coconut Cake

Bake one box butter recipe cake mix as directed on box. Split layers. Spread with frosting.

Frosting:

2 c. sour cream   2 boxes powdered sugar
2 c. fresh coconut

Mix all together and spread on cake while warm. Better if set 2 or 3 days in refrigerator.

Chrissi Bacon

Coconut Cake with Cream Cheese Frosting

1 pkg. yellow cake mix	1 pkg. instant vanilla pie filling
1 1/3 c. water	4 eggs
1/4 c. oil	2 c. coconut

Mix all except coconut; mix for 4 minutes. Add coconut and pour in 3 pans. Bake at 350 degrees for 30 or 35 minutes.

Coconut Cream Cheese Frosting

4 Tbsp. margarine	2 c. coconut
1-8 oz. cream cheese	2 tsp. milk
3 1/2 c. powdered sugar	1/2 tsp. vanilla

Melt margarine in skillet and toast coconut if you want to put frosting on cake.

Bernell Cole

Deep Dark Chocolate Cake

1 1/3 c. all purpose flour	2 c. sugar
3/4 c. cocoa	1 1/2 tsp. baking soda
1 1/2 tsp. baking powder	1 tsp. salt
2 eggs	1 c. milk
1/2 c. oil	2 tsp. vanilla
1 c. boiling water	

Combine dry ingredients. Add remaining ingredients except water; beat 2 minutes at medium speed. Remove from mixer and stir in water (batter will be thin). Pour into greased and floured pans and bake at 350 degrees.

2 8-9 inch pans 30-35 min.	1 13x9 inch pan 35-40 min.

Cool 10 minutes and remove from pans. Cool completely then frost.

Butter Cream Frosting

6 Tbsp. margarine	1/2 c. cocoa
2 2/3 cup powdered sugar	1/2 c. milk
1 tsp. vanilla	

Cream margarine in small bowl. Add cocoa and sugar, alternating with milk. Beat to spreading consistency. Add milk if necessary. Makes about 2 cups.

Jodi Slade

Dirt Cake

1 lg. pkg. oreo cookies (30)	1 sm. vanilla instant pudding
8 oz. cream cheese	1 stick butter
1 c. powdered sugar	1 1/2 c. milk
1-12 oz. cool whip	

Crush cookies in food processor or blender, fine (will resemble top soil). Mix cream cheese, butter and sugar; set aside. Beat pudding, milk; stir in cheese mixture; fold in cool whip. Layer cookies with mixture, ending with cookies on top. Chill and serve with artificial flower in pot.

It's definitely a conversation piece.

Fluffy White Frosting

1 1/2 c. white karo syrup	3 egg whites
1-2 tsp. vanilla	3 or 4 drops almond extract

Bring syrup to boiling. Beat egg whites until fluffy. Pour hot syrup in gradually while beating egg whites. Add flavoring. Continue beating until cool and of right consistency to spread. Will frost three layers.

Anna Lee Little

Fresh Apple Cake

2 c. apples (diced)
1 egg
1 1/2 c. flour
1 tsp. soda
1/2 c. coconut

1 c. sugar
1/2 c. cooking oil
1/2 tsp. salt
1 c. nuts
1 tsp. vanilla

Pour sugar over apples; stir and let set 30 minutes. Mix in other ingredients until well blended. Bake at 350 degrees for one hour.

Twana Miller

Fresh Apple Cake with Hot Sauce

2 c. diced peeled apples
1 egg
1 1/2 tsp. cinnamon
1/2 c. walnuts

1 c. sugar
1 c. flour
1 tsp. soda

Mix sugar with apples and let stand until sugar is dissolved (just a few minutes). Add egg and beat well, sift dry ingredients together and stir into apple mixture. Add nuts. Pour into 8" square baking pan and bake at 375 degrees for 40 minutes. Immediately cover with Hot Sauce.

Hot Sauce:

1/2 c. brown sugar
2 Tbsp. flour
1/4 c. margarine

1/2 c. granulated sugar
1 c. water
1 tsp. vanilla

Cook sugars, flour, and water until clear. Add margarine and vanilla. Stir until margarine is melted. Pour sauce over cake while both are hot.

JoAnn Flynn

Heavenly Hash Cake

2 sticks oleo, melted
2 c. sugar
1 1/2 c. flour
Dash of salt

4 Tbsp. cocoa
4 eggs
1 c. nuts

Combine and mix well. Pour into greased pan. Bake at 350 degrees for 25 minutes. Cover top of cake with miniature marshmallows. Return to oven until melted. Cool in pan.

Icing:

4 Tbsp. cocoa
1 box of powdered sugar

1 stick soft oleo
4 Tbsp. evaporated milk

Mix butter and cocoa. Add sugar and milk. Spread over cooled cake.

Twana Miller

58

Lemon Jello Cake

1 box of yellow cake mix   1 pkg. lemon Jello

Dissolve jello in 3/4 c. hot water and let cool; add to cake mixture. Mix well and add 3/4 c. wesson oil and 2 Tbsp. of lemon extract. Mix well and add 4 eggs one at a time.Grease and flour pan (an Angel Food cake pan is good to use). Bake 50 minutes in 350 degree oven.

Anna Lee Little

Mandarin Orange Cake

1 yellow cake mix (Duncan Hines)   4 eggs

1 can mandarin oranges (put the whole can in)   3/4 c. oil

Mix all the ingredients above.
Bake at 350 degrees until done.

Frosting:

1-20 oz. can crushed pineapple (drained)   1 box vanilla pudding mix
1 box cool whip (8 oz.)

Mix the pineapple and vanilla pudding mix then add cool whip.

Eva Haley

Mayonnaise Cake

2 c. flour   1 c. sugar
1/2 tsp. salt   1 1/2 tsp. soda
1/3 c. cocoa

Mix. Add 1 c. water and 1 tsp. vanilla. Add 2/3 c. salad dressing.
Bake at 350 degrees for 35 to 45 minutes.

Bonnie Vandermolen

Milky Wonder Cake

6 Milky Way Bars or 13 fun-size bars 1 c. butter (2 sticks)
2 c. sugar   4 eggs
2 1/2 c. sifted all purpose flour   1/2 tsp. baking soda
1 1/4 c. buttermilk   1 tsp. vanilla
1 c. chopped nuts

Melt bars and 1/2 c. butter in saucepan over very low heat. Beat remaining 1/2 c. butter and sugar in medium size bowl until fluffy. Add eggs, one at a time, beat well. Add flour and baking soda alternately with buttermilk; stir until smooth. Add melted candy, mixing well. Stir in vanilla and nuts. Pour batter into greased and floured Bundt or ten-inch tube pan. Bake in moderate oven (350) 1 hour and 20 minutes, or until top springs back when lightly touched with fingertip. (Top will be quite dark.) Cool in pan on wire rack 10 minutes. Remove from pan, cool completely. Frost, if you wish.
Note: You may use Snicker Bars instead of the Milky Way Bars and nuts.

Connie Boyle

59

Mississippi Mud Cake

2 c. sugar
1/3 c. cocoa
4 eggs
2 c. nuts
1 1/2 c. plain flour
2 sticks butter
pinch salt
1/2 jar marshmallow cream

(Make own chocolate icing)

Mix all dry ingredients together except marshmallow cream and frosting. Bake in buttered long baking dish 350 degrees until done. While warm, spread marshmallow cream over top. Spread chocolate frosting. Cut into squares.

Anna Lee Little

No Name Cake

Crust:
1 white cake mix
1 stick of butter
1 egg

Topping:
1 box powdered sugar
8 oz. cream cheese
2 eggs

Bake at 350 degrees for 40 minutes.

Sharon Qualls

No Bake Fruit Cake

Heat and melt:
1 c. orange juice
1/2 lg. pkg. miniature marshmallows
1-14 oz. pkg. graham cracker crumbs
1 c. candied pineapple
2 c. pecans
1 c. candied cherries

Line loaf pan or bundt pan with waxed paper or spray with pam. Mix ingredients together and pack in pan. Refrigerate at least one month before serving.

Joey Smith

Oatmeal Cake

1 c. oatmeal
1 c. brown sugar
1/2 c. shortening
1 1/2 c. flour
1 tsp. cinnamon
1 1/2 c. hot water
1 c. white sugar
2 eggs
1 tsp. soda
1/2 tsp. salt

Pour hot water over oatmeal. Set aside. Cream sugars and shortening . Beat in eggs. Sift together remaining dry ingredients and add alternately with oatmeal to sugar mixture. Pour into greased 9x13 pan. Bake at 350 degrees for 25-30 minutes (325 degrees for glass pan).

Icing:

1 stick margarine   2 Tbsp. Evaporated milk
1 c. brown sugar   1 c. coconut
1 c. nuts   1 tsp. vanilla

Boil margarine, milk and sugar for one minute. Remove from heat and add last 3 ingredients. Spread on cake. Toast in broiler until bubbles (burns easily).

Paula McLarty

Peanut Butter Pudding Cake

1 pkg. (2-layer size) yellow cake mix 1 Tbsp. sugar
1 pkg. (4-serving size) vanilla instant pudding and pie filling
4 eggs   1 c. water
1/4 c. oil   1 c. crunchy peanut butter

Combine all ingredients in large mixer bowl. Blend; then beat at medium speed of electric mixer for 4 minutes. Pour into greased and floured 10-inch tube pan. Bake at 350 degrees for 55 to 60 minutes or until cake springs back when lightly pressed. Cool in pan about 15 minutes. Remove from pan and finish cooling on rack. Top with prepared whipped topping and banana slices, if desired. For high altitude areas, use large eggs; add 1/3 c. all purpose flour; increase water to 1 1/2 c.; and bake at 375 dgrees for 50 minutes.

Johnnie Whitten

Pineapple Sheet Cake

2 c. sugar   1/4 c. oil
2 eggs   2 tsp. soda
2 c. flour   1 lg. can crushed pineapple

Mix all and bake in a long pan at 350 for 30 minutes.
Topping:
1 can (sm.) Pet milk   1 stick oleo
1 c. sugar

Boil slowly for 7 minutes then add 1 c. coconut and (1 c. nuts if you want to). Pour over cake while hot.

Bernell Cole

Post Office Cake

1 Duncan Hines butter cake mix   1/2 c. oil
2 eggs   1 can mandarin oranges with juice

Mix and bake in 3 layers.

Icing:

1 lg. cool whip   1 box vanilla instant pudding mix
2 can crushed pineapple (drained)

Mix and spread between layers - refrigerate.

Connie Boyle

Quick Fudge Icing

1/2 c. sugar
1 Tbsp. light corn syrup
1/2 tsp. vanilla
1/4 c. milk

1 Tbsp. butter
1/4 tsp. salt
2 Tbsp. cocoa
3/4 - 1 c. powdered sugar

Mix all except vanilla and powdered sugar; boil for 3 minutes; beat in vanilla and powdered sugar.

Linda Waters

Rhubarb Pudding Cake

1 cake mix (white or yellow)
3 to 4 c. sugar

3 to 4 c. Rhubarb (cut in sm. pieces)
3 c. boiling water

Preheat oven to 375. Mix the cake mix as directed on the box. Pour the rhubarb evenly over the cake mix. Then pour the sugar evenly on the rhurbarb. Finally pour the boiling water on top. Let bake 40 to 45 minutes.

Alberta Reed

Sock-It-To-Me Cake

1 pkg. butter cake mix (dry)
1/2 c. crisco oil
4 eggs

1 c. sour cream
1/4 c. sugar
1/4 c. water

Filling:

1 c. chopped pecans
2 tsp. cinnamon

2 Tbsp. brown sugar
2 Tbsp. cake mix (dry)

Glaze:

1 c. powdered sugar

2 Tbsp. milk

In large bowl, blend together cake mix, sour cream, oil, sugar, water and eggs. Beat at high speed for 2 minutes. Pour 2/3 batter in greased and floured tube pan. Combine filling ingredients and sprinkle over batter in pan. Spread remaining batter over filling mixture. Bake in 375 degree oven for 45-55 minutes. Cool cake for 25 minutes then remove from pan. Drizzle glaze over top of cake.

Cindy Binder

Strawberry Angel Food Fluff

1 angel food cake
1 can Eagle Brand milk
1-15 oz. jar strawberry glaze

1-8 oz. cool whip, thawed
1/4 c. lemon juice
1 qt. strawberries, chopped

Combine cool whip and Eagle Brand milk; stir. Add lemon juice, stir until thickened. Add 2/3 of the glaze and 2/3 of the strawberries. Cut cake into layers and spread filling between layers and on top. Mix remaining glaze and strawberries together; spread on top of cake also. Keep in refrigerator.

Linda Campbell

Surprise Chocolate Cake

1 chocolate cake mix

Mix according to package directions. Spread half of cake mixture in 13x9 pan. Mix the following in separate bowl:

1-8 oz. cream cheese
1 egg
1 c. chopped nuts

1/3 c. sugar
1-6 oz. pkg. chocolate chips

Drop this cream cheese mixture over the top of the cake mixture. Then cover the cream cheese mixture with the rest of the cake batter. Bake at 350 degrees.

Icing:

1 stick margarine
6 Tbsp. milk
1 tsp. vanilla

4 Tbsp. cocoa
1 box confectioners sugar

Heat margarine, cocoa, and milk till it comes to a boil. Remove from heat, add sugar and vanilla. Beat until smooth and has spreading consistency.

Allison Totten

Two Egg Cake

1 3/4 c. self-rising flour
1/2 c. butter or shortening or 1 stick margarine, melted
2 eggs, unbeaten
1 tsp. vanilla
Cook at 375 degrees.

1 c. plus 2 Tbsp. sugar

2/3 c. milk

Sharon Qualls

Upsidedown Pineapple Cake

2 egg yolks
1/4 c. pineapple juice or boiling water
3/4 c. flour (self-rising)
2 stiff beaten egg whites

3/4 c. sugar

1/2 tsp. vanilla

Beat egg yolks until thick and yellow. Gradually add sugar and continue beating. Add pineapple juice; mix well. Add dry ingredients and vanilla. Place brown sugar and pineapple in bottom of iron skillet. Fold in egg whites. Bake in 325 degree oven about 1 hour.

Cindy Binder

White Coconut Cake

3 c. sifted cake flour
1/2 tsp. salt
1/2 tsp. vinegar
1 c. (2 sticks) butter, softened
1 c. milk

3 tsp. baking powder
1 c. egg whites (about 8)
2 c. sugar
1 tsp. vanilla
1 pkg. (7 oz.) flaked coconut

Grease and line bottoms of two 9 x 1 1/2-inch cake pans with wax paper; grease paper. Sift flour, baking powder and salt onto sheet of wax paper. Preheat oven to 350 degrees. Beat egg whites in a bowl until foamy. Beat in vinegar, then 1 c. of the sugar, 1 Tbsp. at a time, until meringue forms soft peaks.

Beat butter in a bowl until creamy. Beat in remaining 1 c. sugar and vanilla. Add sifted dry ingredients alternately with milk, stirring between each addition until batter is smooth. Carefully fold in meringue. Pour batter into pans. Bake in preheated oven for 30 minutes or until centers spring back when pressed with fingertip. Cool on wire rack 5 minutes. Remove from pans; peel off wax paper; cool completely.

Frost with Boiled White Frosting. Sprinkle generously with coconut.

Boiled White Frosting:

2 c. sugar
2 Tbsp. light corn syrup
4 eggs
1 tsp. vanilla

1/2 c. water
Dash salt
1/2 tsp. vinegar

Combine sugar, water, corn syrup and salt in a pan. Cook over medium heat, stirring until sugar is dissolved. Wash sugar crystals from side of pan with a pastry brush dipped in water. Clip candy thermometer to side of pan. Boil syrup to the soft ball stage (240 degrees on candy thermometer) or until a fork, when dipped into the syrup and held above the pan, will form a thread. Beat egg whites until foamy. Add vinegar; beat until stiff peaks form. Pour the syrup in a thin stream into the beaten whites while beating the mixture. Beat until frosting is thick and forms soft peaks; beat in vanilla.

LaTina Kurtley

Best Oatmeal Cookies

3/4 c. shortening	1 c. firmly packed brown sugar
1/2 c. granualted sugar	1 egg
1/4 c. water	1 tsp. vanilla
3 cups oats (uncooked)	1 c. all purpose flour
1 tsp. salt	1/2 tsp. soda

Preheat oven to 350 degrees. Beat shortening, sugars, egg, water and vanilla until creamy. Add combined remaining ingredients and mix well. Drop by rounded teaspoon full onto greased cookie sheet. Bake 8-12 minutes.

Cyndi Engles

Brown Sugar Cookies

1/2 c. butter or shortening	1 egg
1/4 c. granulated sugar	3/4 cup firmly packed brown sugar
1 tsp. vanilla	1 c. sifted flour
1/2 tsp. baking soda	1/2 tsp. salt

Beat butter, egg, sugar and vanilla until light and fluffy. Add dry ingredients; blend well. Drop from teaspoon onto ungreased baking sheet, 2 inches apart; with fork, press down a little before baking in oven at 350 degrees for 8 to 10 minutes. Makes 3 to 4 dozen cookies.

Ruthel Pilkington

Brownie Delight

1 pkg. brownie mix	1 pkg. chocolate chips
1 c. chopped pecans	1 pkg. caramels

Follow directions on brownie mix box and bake. While brownies are baking, heat caramels in double boiler until melted. When brownies are down, take out and pour caramel on top. Sprinkle with chocolate chips and pecans. Let cool and cut into squares.

Chrissi Bacon

Buffalo Chip Cookies

2 cups (4 sticks) melted oleo	2 cups packed light brown sugar
2 cups white sugar	

Stir in:

4 eggs (be sure oleo is cooled)	2 tsp. vanilla
2 cups quick-cooking oats	2 cups corn flakes
4 cups plain flour	2 tsp. baking powder
2 tsp. soda	

Then add:

1-6 oz. pkg. chocolate chips.	2 cups pecans

(you may put anything you want in them-coconut, sunflower seeds, raisins, M&M's, etc.)

Use an ice cream scoop to put cookie dough onto a large cookie sheet. (about 6 to a sheet). Bake at 325 degrees for about 17 minutes on the highest rack in the oven. Makes about 35 cookies.

Ann Horn

Chewy Chocolate Oatmeal Cookies

1/2 c. Hershey's cocoa
1 (14-oz) can Eagle Brand Milk (not evaporated milk)
2 eggs, beaten
1 1/2 cups quick-cooking oats
1/4 tsp. salt
1 (10-oz.) pkg. Hershey's Vanilla Milk chips or 1 (12-oz. pkg. Reeses
Peanut Butter chips

1/2 c. margarine or butter, melted

2 tsp. vanilla
1 c. biscuit baking mix

Preheat overn to 350 degrees. In large bowl, stir cocoa and margarine until smooth. Stir in remaining ingredients until well blended. Let dough stand 10 minutes; drop by heaping teaspoonfuls onto lightly greased baking sheet. Bake 7 to 9 minutes or until set (do not overbake). Cool 5 minutes; remove from baking sheets. Cool completely. Store tightly covered. Makes about 4 dozen.

Holly Arnold

Chocolate Chip Cookies From Bloomingdales

Cream:
    2 cups butter
    2 cups brown sugar

2 cups sugar

Add:
    4 eggs

2 tsp. vanilla

Mix:
    4 cups flour
    (Mix in small amounts in blender until powder forms)

5 cups oatmeal

Add:
    1 tsp. salt
    2 tsp. baking soda

2 tsp. baking powder

Mix all ingredients and add 24 oz. pkg. of Chocolate chips and 1 (8 oz.) Hershey bar (coursely grated). Make golf ball size and drop onto ungreased cookie sheet 2 inches apart. Bake at 375 degrees for 5-6 minutes. Do not overbake. Makes 142 cookies

Mrs. Janet Schwartz

Chocolate Chip Peanut Butter Cookies

2 1/2 cups flour
1/2 tsp. baking soda
1 cup peanut butter
1 cup brown sugar, packed
1/2 cup chocolate chips

1/2 tsp. salt
1 cup butter
1 cup white sugar
2 eggs

Mix flour, salt and baking soda then set aside. Mix butter and peanut butter. Add both kinds of sugar; mix well. Add eggs and beat well. Stir flour mixture into peanut butter mixture. Drop dough from teaspoon on baking pan. Flatten with a fork. Bake at 375 degrees for 10-15 minutes.

Julie Barnes

Chocolate Covered Peanut Butter Balls

2 sticks butter   1 1/2 cup peanut butter
1 box powdered sugar

Soften butter, add peanut butter, add powdered sugar. Blend well. Roll into balls. Dip in Coating: 1/2 cake parafin and 1 pkg. of chocolate chips (melted).

Lula Qualls

Chocolate Fudge

4 cups sugar   1 cup Pet Milk
2 sticks butter   1 pint marshmellow cream
2 pkgs. (6 oz.) chocolate chips   1/2 cup nuts

Using a heavy container, boil sugar, butter and milk until the soft ball stage. Remove from stove and add chocolate chips, marshmellow cream and nuts.

Sherry Clark

Chocolate Fudge

2 cups. sugar   4 tbsp. cocoa
1/3 cup syrup   1/2 cup milk
2 tbsp. butter   1 tsp. vanilla

Mix sugar and cocoa, add syrup and milk. Cook in saucepan over medium heat stirring to keep from burning until it forms a soft ball when dropped in cold water. Remove from heat, add vanilla and butter. Let cool. Beat until smooth and thick. Pour on buttered platter and cut into squares.

Cora Lou Davis

Chocolate Nut Brownies

1 (12 oz.) pkg. Hershey's Semi-Sweet Chocolate Chips
1/4 c. margarine or butter]   1 egg, beaten
2 cups biscuit baking mix   1 tsp. vanilla
1 (14 oz.) can Eagle Brand Milk (not evaporated milk)
1 to 1 1/2 cup chopped pecans   Confectioners' sugar

Preheat oven to 350 degrees. In large saucepan, over low heat, melt 1 cup chips with margarine; remove from heat. Add biscuit mix, sweetened condensed milk, egg and vanilla. Stir in nuts and remaining chips. Turn into well-greased 13x9 baking pan. Bake 20 to 25 minutes or until brownies begin to pull away from sides of pan. Cool. Sprinkle with confectioners' sugar. Cut into bars. Store tightly covered. Makes 24 to 36 brownies.

Holly Arnold

Chocolate Pecan Bars

1 1/4 c. unsifted flour
1/2 c. cocoa
1 (14 oz.) can Eagle Brand Milk
2 tsp. vanilla
1 c. confectioners' sugar
1 c. cold margarine
1 egg
1 1/2 c. pecans-chopped (optional)

In a large bowl mix flour, sugar and cocoa. Cut margarine in until crumbly. Press firm on bottom of 13x9 baking pan. Bake 15 minutes at 350 degrees. Meanwhile, beat Eagle Brand, egg and vanilla. Spread evenly over crust. Bake 25 minutes or until light brown. Cool. Cut into bars. Store in refrigerator.

Sandra Williams

Chocolate Peanut Butter Clusters

Power level: High (100%)   Total cooking time: 3 to 4 minutes

1 pkg. (6 oz.) chocolate morsels
1 pkg. (12 oz.) peanut butter morsels
1 pkg. (12 oz.) salted Spanish peanuts

1. Combine morsels in a 2 quart casserole. Microwave on High (100%) for 3 to 4 minutes or until melted. Stir halfway through cooking.
2. Stir in peanuts.
3. Drop by teaspoons onto waxed paper. Let set until firm. Store in airtight container. Yield: 4 to 4 1/2 dozen,

Julie Johnson

Congo Bars

2 c. light brown sugar
3/4 c. margarine
2 1/4 c. plain flour
1 tsp. salt
3 eggs
1-small pkg. chocolate chips
1 tsp. soda

Mix all together and pour in a long greased baking dish and bake at 350 degrees. Cool and cut into squares.

Janta Downing

Double Chocolate Oatmeal Cookies

1 1/2 c. sugar
1 egg
1 tsp. vanilla
1/3 c. cocoa
1/2 tsp. salt
1 pkg. chocolate chips
1 c. margarine or butter (softened)
1/4 c. water
1 1/4 c. all purpose flour
1/2 tsp. baking soda
3 c. quick cooking oats

Heat over to 350 degrees. Mix sugar, margarine, egg, water and vanilla. Stir in remaining ingredients. Drop dough by rounded teaspoonfuls about 2 inches apart onto ungreased cookie sheet. Bake until almost no indentation remains when touched (10-12 minutes). Remove from cookie sheet. Makes about 5 dozen cookies.

Debbie Watkins

Fantasy Fudge

3 c. sugar
2/3 c. evaporated milk
1 jar marshmallow cream
1 tsp. vanilla

3/4 c. margarine
1 (12 oz.) pkg. chocolate chips
1 c. nuts

Combine sugar, margarine and milk. Cook to a full boil and continue cooking for 5 minutes over medium heat. Remove from heat and stir in chips until melted. Add marshmellow cream, nuts and vanilla.

Kristie Robison

Fudgy Chocolate Cookie Bars

1 3/4 c. unsifted flour
1/4 c. Hershey's cocoa
1 (12 oz.) pkg. Hershey's chocolate chips
1 (14 oz.) can Eagle Brand Milk
1 c. chopped nuts

3/4 c. confectioners' sugar
1 c. cold margarine or butter

1 tsp. vanilla

Preheat oven to 350 degrees. In medium bowl, combine flour, sugar and cocoa; cut in margarine until crumbly (mixture will be dry). Press firmly on bottom of 13x9 baking pan. Bake 15 minutes. Meanwhile, in medium saucepan, over medium heat, melt 1 cup chips with sweetened condensed milk and vanilla. Pour evenly over prepared crust. Top with nuts and remaining 1 cup chips; press down firmly. Bake 20 minutes or until set. Cook. Chill if desired. Cut into bars. Store tightly covered. Makes 24 to 36 bars.

Holly Arnold

Funfetti Cookies

1 pkg. Pillsbury Plus Funfetti cake mix
1/3 c. oil   2 eggs
1 can Pillsbury Pink Vanilla Fun Frosting

Heat oven to 375 degrees. In large bowl, combine cake mix, oil and eggs. Stir by hand until thoroughly moistened. Stir in candy bits from cake mix. Shape dough into 1 inch balls. Place 2 inches apart on ungreased cookie sheet. Flatten to 1/4 inch thickness with bottom of glass dipped in flour. Bake for 6 to 8 minutes or until edges are light golden brown. Cool 1 minute. Remove from cookie sheet. Immediately sprinkle each with candy bits from frosting. Store in tightly covered container. 3 dozen cookies.

Shana Ward

Helen's Fudge - 5 Pounds

4 cups sugar
3 (6 oz.) pkgs. chocolate chips
2 tsp. vanilla

1 large can Carnation milk
1/2 lb. butter
30 large marshmallows-cut up or
1 (10 oz.) pkg. miniature
marshmallows

2 cups nuts

Cook sugar and milk. Stir occasionally. When mixture comes to a full boil - time for 11 minutes. Remove from heat, add chocolate chips, butter vanilla and marshmallows. Beat well, add nuts and beat some more. Pour into pan.

Helen Cushman

Mama's Oatmeal Cookies

3/4 c. butter
1 c. sugar
1 1/2 c. flour
1 tsp. cloves
1/2 c. raisins

3/4 tsp. soda
1 tsp. cinnamon
1 c. rolled oats
1/2 c. chopped nuts
2 eggs

Mix all together and drop by spoonfuls on a greased sheet and bake in moderate oven for 10 to 15 minutes.

Mona Ray

Million Dollar Cookies

1 c. flour
1/2 tsp. vanilla
1 c. chopped nuts

3/4 c. sugar
1 stick butter

Mix all ingredients well. Roll into small balls; place on a cookie sheet and flatten with a glass, which has been dipped in sugar. Bake at 350 degrees for 10 minutes. Variations: you may add chopped candied cherries or coconut.

Becky James

Million Dollar Fudge

4 1/2 c. granulated sugar
3 Tbsp. butter
1-12 oz. pkg. chocolate chips
3-4 oz. pkgs. German sweet chocolate chips
1 pt. of marshmallow cream

Dash of salt
1-14 oz. can condensed milk

2 or more c. English walnuts

Combine first four ingredients in a large pan. Cook over medium heat stirring constantly until mixture comes to a full boil. Boil 6 minutes exactly. Remove from heat and stir in other ingredients quickly.

Note: Milk now is in 13 oz. cans, you must add 1 more oz. Also, regular chocolate chips can replace German chocolate chips.

Maleta Engle

M&M Cookies

1/2 c. butter
1 pkg. chocolate chip
1 can Eagle Brand milk

1 1/2 c. graham cracker crumbs
1/2 pkg. coconut
1 lg. bag M&M's

Mix all ingredients and bake at 350 degrees for 20 to 25 minutes.

Sandy Arnold

Mock Heath Bars

2 sticks real butter (1 cup); do not substitute w/margarine
1 c. sugar   saltine crackers
pecans, chopped   12 oz. chocolate chips

Line 9x12 cookie sheet with foil, then spray with Pam. Place crackers on foil salty side up. Melt butter and sugar together; boil 3 minutes (time this - do not over or undercook). Pour butter/sugar mixture over crackers. Bake at 350 degrees for 5 minutes. Take out and pour chocolate chips on top and spread out. Sprinkle with pecans. Place in refrigerator. Break into pieces.

Paula McLarty

No Bake Cookies

2 c. sugar   1/2 c. cocoa
1/2 c. milk   1 stick butter

Combine and bring to a boil. Cook 2 minutes. Remove from heat; add 1 c. peanut butter; stir until melted. Add 3 c. quick cooking oatmeal. Drop by teaspoon onto wax paper.

Sandy Arnold

No Bake Cookies

1/2 c. margarine   1/2 c. cocoa
1/4 c. milk   2 c. sugar
3 c. quick oats   1 tsp. vanilla
1 c. peanut butter   1/2 c. nuts (optional)

In double boiler mix margarine, milk, sugar, and cocoa. Bring to a boil for 2 minutes. Stir in oats and peanut butter, vanilla and nuts. Spoon and drop on slightly buttered pan. Let sit for 20 minutes and serve.

Sandra Williams

Old Fashioned Christmas Cookies

2 c. sugar
1 c. (2 sticks) oleo or butter
6 Tbsp. milk
4 c. flour
1/2 tsp. salt

1/4 c. light brown sugar
2 eggs
2 tsp. vanilla
2 tsp. baking powder

Cream butter and sugar. Add eggs, milk, and vanilla. Beat well, sift dry ingredients. Add batter mixture. Beat well; chill. Roll out and cut. Bake in 350 degree oven for 10-12 minutes.

Elizabeth Walker

Peanut Butter Cookies

1 c. butter or margarine
1 c. sugar
2 eggs, beaten
3 c. flour
2 tsp. baking soda

1 tsp. vanilla
1 c. brown sugar
1 c. peanut butter
Pinch of salt

Cream together butter or margarine, vanilla, and sugars. Add eggs and beat well. Stir in peanut butter and then sift dry ingredients. Form into little balls. Place on a greased cookie sheet; press down with the prongs of a fork. Bake at 375 degrees for 10 minutes. Makes 5 dozen.

Twana Miller

Peanut Butter Fudge

2 c. sugar   2/3 c. cream

Cook until soft boil stage. Then add vanilla and 1 c. peanut butter and 1 c. marshmallow cream.

Maleta Engle

Playing Hooky Cookies

Preheat oven to 350. Lightly grease a large cookie sheet. Cream together in a large mixing bowl until light and fluffy: 1/2 c. soft butter and 1/2 c. crunchy peanut butter. Add gradually to butter mixture: 1/2 c. granulated sugar and 1/2 c. brown sugar. Sift and mix well: 1 c. flour, 1 tsp. vanilla, and a pinch of salt. Flour hands lightly and roll dough into small balls (about size of walnuts). Place on cookie sheet about 2 inches apart. Flatten dough with a floured fork. Bake 12-15 minutes. Remove cookies with turner. Cool on wire rack.

Angie Sharp

Salted Peanut Chews

Crust:

1 1/2 c. plain flour	2/3 c. firmly packed brown sugar
1/2 tsp. baking powder	1/2 tsp. salt
1/4 tsp. baking soda	1 tsp. vanilla
1/2 c. margarine or butter, softened	2 egg yolks
3 c. miniature marshmallows	

Topping:

2/3 c. corn syrup	1/4 c. margarine or butter
2 tsp. vanilla	
12 oz. pkg. (2 cups) peanut butter chips	
2 c. rice crispie cereal	2 c. salted peanuts

Heat oven to 350 degrees. Lightly spoon flour into measuring cup; level off. In large bowl, combine all crust ingredients except marshmallows on low speed until crumbly. Press firmly in bottom of ungreased 13x9 inch pan. Bake at 350 degrees for 12 to 15 minutes or until light golden brown. Immediatley sprinkle with marshmallows. Return to oven for 1 to 2 minutes or until marshmallows just begin to puff. Cool while preparing topping.

In large saucepan heat corn syrup, margarine, vanilla and peanut butter chips just until chips are melted and mixture is smooth, stirring constantly. Remove from heat; stir in cereal and nuts. Immediately spoon warm topping over marshmallows and spread to cover. Refrigerate until firm; cut into bars - 36 bars.

Cheryl Watkins

Snickerdoodles

1 1/2 c. sugar	1 tsp. vanilla
1/2 c. margarine or butter, softened	2 eggs
2 3/4 c. all purpose flour	1 tsp. cream of tartar
1/2 tsp. baking soda	1/4 tsp. salt
2 Tbsp. sugar	2 tsp. cinnamon

Heat oven to 400 degrees. In a large bowl, beat 1 1/2 c. sugar and margarine until fluffy. Add vanilla and eggs; beat well. Lightly spoon flour into measuring cup; level off. Add flour, cream of tartar, baking soda and salt; mix well. In small bowl, combine 2 Tbsp. sugar and cinnamon. Shape dough into 1 inch balls; roll balls in sugar/cinnamon mixture. Place 2 inches apart onto greased cookie sheets. Bake at 400 degrees for 8-10 minutes or until set. Remove cookies from sheet. Makes 8 dozen.

Linda Taylor

Susan Brownies

2 c. sugar	3/4 c. wesson oil
3 eggs	3 Tbsp. water
1 1/2 tsp. salt	5 Tbsp. cocoa
1 1/2 c. sifted flour	1 tsp. vanilla

Sift flour and salt together. Mix sugar and wesson oil. Add eggs, vanilla and cocoa. Then add flour mixture. Bake at 350 for 20-25 minutes.

Karen Cushman

The Ultimate Chocolate Chip Cookie

3/4 c. butter flavor Crisco
1 1/4 c. firmly packed brown sugar   2 Tbsp. milk
1 tsp. vanilla   1 egg
1 3/4 c. all purpose flour   1 tsp. salt
3/4 tsp. baking soda   1 c. semi-sweet chocolate chips
1 c. pecan pieces

Heat oven to 375. Cream crisco, brown sugar, milk and vanilla in large bowl. Blend till creamy. Blend in egg. Combine flour, salt and baking soda. Add to creamed mixture; gradually stir in chocolate chips and nuts. Drop by rounded tablespoonfuls (about 2 tablespoons) of dough 3 inches apart on ungreased baking sheet. Bake at 375 for 8 to 10 minutes.

Cyndi Engles

Yogi Balls

4 Tbsp. butter   1 c. sugar
1 egg, beaten   1 Tbsp. vanilla
2 c. Rice Krispies   2 c. pecans
box of dates   coconut

Melt butter in heavy skillet; add sugar, egg, and dates. Cook until dates are dissolved. Remove from heat and add pecans, Rice Krispies, and vanilla. Make out into balls and roll in coconut.

Maleta Engle

Almond Bark

1 lb. pure chocolate (milk, white or dark)
1 c. almonds

Place chocolate in a 2 qt. casserole (if solid break into pieces). Microwave on medium for 3 to 5 minutes or until melted. Stir halfway through cooking. Stir in almonds. Pour onto waxed paper. Spread to 1/4 inch thickness. Cool until hard. Break into pieces. Store in airtight container.

Julie Johnson

Almond Bark Mix

2 c. rice krispies
2 c. broken pretzel sticks
2 lbs. white chocolate (or) Almond Bark
2 heaping Tbsp. peanut butter
2 c. roasted spanish peanuts

Melt almond bark in double boiler. Add peanut butter. Mix in other ingredients. Drop by tsp. onto wax paper.

Kim Sage

Broken Glass Candy

3 3/4 c. sugar
1 c. water
1 1/4 c. white syrup
2 Tbsp. cinnamon oil

Boil first 3 ingredients until hard rock stage - remove from heat - add food coloring and cinnamon oil. Pour on pan sprayed with pam - let set and harden.

Rena Bowser

Caramel Corn

1 c. margarine
1/2 c. light corn syrup
1 tsp. vanilla
2 c. brown sugar, packed
1 tsp. soda
6-8 qt. popped corn

Melt margarine in a large sauce pan. Stir in brown sugar, corn syrup and salt. Bring to a boil, stirring constantly. Boil without stirring for 5 minutes. Remove from heat; add soda and vanilla. Gradually pour over popped corn in a large roasting pan, mixing thoroughly. Bake in 250 degree oven for 1 hour, stirring every 15 minutes. Remove from oven and cool completely. Break apart and store in tightly covered container. Makes 5 quarts. Peanuts may be added before coating with syrup.

Linda Taylor

Cornflake Treats

1 c. corn syrup, light or dark
1 1/2 c. peanut butter
4 c. cornflakes
1 c. sugar
1 tsp. vanilla

Boil corn syrup and sugar just until sugar dissolves. Take off stove. Stir in peanut butter and vanilla. Add cornflakes. Mix until all cornflakes are coated with mixture. Drop from teaspoon onto wax paper. Allow to cool. Makes about 50 cookies.

Pat Smith

Easy Caramels

1 c. butter   1 lb. brown sugar
1 dash salt   1 c. light corn syrup
1-15 oz. can sweetened condensed milk
1 tsp. vanilla

Melt butter in heavy 3 qt. saucepan. Add brown sugar and salt. Blend in corn syrup and sweetened condensed milk. Cook and stir over medium heat until candy makes firm ball, about 12 to 15 minutes. Remove from heat, stir in vanilla. Cool, cut into small squares. Makes 2 1/2 pounds candy.
This is good for caramel apples and will do 25 or 30 apples.

Cora Lou Davis

English Toffee

1/2 c. finely chopped pecans   1 c. butter
1 c. firmly packed light brown sugar   1/2 c. semi-sweet chocolate chips

Sprinkle 1/4 c. pecans over bottom of lightly buttered 9-inch pan. Set aside. Combine butter and brown sugar in heavy saucepan. Cook over medium heat, stirring constantly, to 295 degrees on a candy thermometer. Pour over pecans. Sprinkle with chocolate chips. Spread evenly when melted. Sprinkle with remaining pecans; press lightly. Cool completely. Break into pieces. Store in a refrigerator in airtight container.

Julie Johnson

Grandma's Peanut Brittle

1 c. sugar   1/2 c. syrup
1/3 c. water

Cook until soft ball stage; add 1 cup peanuts and cook until golden color. Remove from heat; add 1 teaspoon soda. Pour on buttered cookie sheet.

Maleta Engle

Hard Candy

3 3/4 c. sugar   1 c. water
1 1/2 c. corn syrup   1 tsp. flavoring oil
Food coloring

Mix sugar, water and syrup in a large saucepan. Boil without stirring to 310 degrees. Remove from heat; add flavoring oil and food coloring. Pour onto lightly buttered cookie sheet to cool. Break into small pieces and store in airtight container.

Debbie Stewart

Millionnaires

1-14 oz. pkg. of caramels   2 Tbsp. milk
2 c. pecans
1-6 oz. pkg. semi-sweet chocolate chips
1/2 block paraffin

Melt caramels and milk in top of double boiler. Beat 2-3 minutes. Add pecans and drop on wax paper. Melt chocolate chips and 1/2 block paraffin. Dip caramel-nut drops into chocolate mixture and return to wax paper.

Anna Qualls

Molasses Taffy

2 c. molasses   1 c. granulated sugar
3/4 c. water   1/8 tsp. soda
4 Tbsp. butter   1/2 tsp. vanilla

Cook the molasses, sugar, and water slowly to the hard ball stage (260 degrees) stirring during the latter part of the cooking to prevent burning. Remove from the fire, add fat, soda, and vanilla and stir enough to mix. Pour into a greased pan and when cool enough to handle, pull it until it becomes light in color. Stretch it into a long rope and cut it with scissors into small pieces.

Leta Engle

Peanut Brittle

1 1/2 c. sugar   1/2 c. white syrup
1/4 c. water   2 c. raw peanuts

Cook in skillet over medium high heat until peanuts pop. (15 min.)
Remove from heat and add 1 heaping tsp. soda. Mix quickly and pour in a buttered long pan or cookie sheet. Let stand until cold. Break into pieces. Store in air tight container or plastic bags.

Cora Lou Davis

Pralines

1 1/2 c. sugar   3/4 c. brown sugar
1/2 c. milk   3/4 stick butter
1 1/2 c. pecans   1 tsp. vanilla

Combine all except vanilla and bring to boil; cook to soft ball stage, stirring constantly. Remove from heat and add vanilla. Stir until mixture thickens, becomes creamy and cloudy and pecans stay suspended in mixture. Spoon on buttered waxed paper. Makes 1-50 depending on size.

Debbie Stewart

Reese's Cups

1 box powdered sugar
1 tsp. vanilla
2 sticks butter, melted
1-12 oz. pkg. chocolate chips

1 1/2 c. peanut butter
3/4 c. graham cracker crumbs

Mix together all ingredients except chocolate chips and press into 9x13 inch pan. Melt the 12 oz. pkg. chocolate chips. Pour over peanut butter mixture. Chill until chocolate hardens.

Sherry Ward

Taffy

2 c. sugar
1 c. light corn syrup
1 tsp. salt
1/4 tsp. any flavoring food color as desired

2 Tbsp. corn starch
3/4 c. water
2 Tbsp. margarine

In a heavy saucepan, mix together sugar and corn starch. Stir in corn syrup, water, salt, and margarine. Place over medium heat and stir until sugar dissolves. Cover pan and bring to a boil for 2 or 3 minutes. Uncover; place thermometer in pan and cook to 266 degrees. Remove from heat and add flavoring and food coloring. Stir gently; pour on a greased pan to cool. When cool enough to handle grease hands and pull until light in color and has a satiny gloss. Pull into a long rope; cut with scissors and wrap in waxed paper square twisting ends. Yields about 50 pieces.

Kim Yager

Miscellaneous

Spring House ~ Evening Shade, Arkansas

Catfish House Mix

1 gallon quartered green tomatoes   1 qt. quartered onions
1 pt. hot peppers cut into 1 in. lengths
1 pt. white vinegar   3 c. sugar
1/4 c. salt

Mix all together, bring to a boil or until tomatoes turn light green. DO NOT BOIL. Gently stir a couple of times. Seal in hot jars.

Barb Johns

Chocolate Gravy

4 Tbsp. cocoa   4 Tbsp. flour
1 1/2 c. sugar   3 c. milk
1 stick of butter

Cook on stove until thick; eat with biscuits. Can add more butter if you like.

Joyce Bradford

Cucumber Pickles

Wash cucumbers and place in a gal. jar
Mix and pour over cucumbers:
     4 c. vinegar   2 Tbsp. alum
     4 Tbsp. salt   3 Tbsp. pickling spices

Pour over cucumbers and let stand 3 weeks. Pour off liquid; slice cucumbers and add 6 c. sugar, stir sugar and let stand for 3 or 4 days.

Renee' Bailey

Family Favorite Barbeque Dip

1 can (8 oz.) tomato sauce   2 Tbsp. brown sugar
1 Tbsp. worcestershire sauce   1 Tbsp. vinegar
1 tsp. prepared mustard   1 tsp. instant minced onion
1/2 tsp. hot pepper sauce   1/8 tsp. instant minced garlic

Combine ingredients in sauce pan. Bring to a boil over medium heat, stirring occasionally. To serve, dip chicken in sauce. Sauce ingredients can be combined in microwave safe bowl. Cook in microwave on high power 2 minutes, stir to blend.

Shana Ward

Fudgesicles

1 sm. package instant chocolate pudding mix
1/4 c. sugar   4 c. milk

Thoroughly mix pudding mix, sugar and milk together. Pour into paper cups, molds or ice cube trays. Freeze for 30 minutes; insert wooden sticks or plastic teaspoons into center of each.

Jan Weatherley

Grandma's Relish

12 cucumbers - 1 in. in diameter (young cucumbers)

4 lg. onions	1/2 c. salt
1 c. vinegar	1 c. sugar
1 Tbsp. mustard seed	1 Tbsp. celery seed
1 Tbsp. ginger	1 tsp. turmeric

Chop onions and cucumbers into small pieces (better chopped by hand). Sprinkle with salt and let stand 1 hour. Rinse quickly with cold water and drain. In large kettle, heat vinegar with other ingredients; bring to boiling stage. Add cucumber and onions quickly. Return to boiling point and boil one minute. Pack immediately into pint jars and seal.

Tammi Bacon

Green Tomato Pickles

1 qt. apple cider vinegar	1/2 c. canning salt
4 c. sugar	1 tsp. black pepper
1 gallon green tomatoes, sliced	1/2 gallon green and red peppers
1/2 gallon onions	2 or 3 pods hot peppers

Cook until they change color and can.

Stella Qualls

Green Tomato Pickles

7 qt. small tomatoes quartered	5 lg. onions
1 c. sliced hot pepper	

Mix together:

1/2 c. salt	4 c. sugar
4 c. vinegar	

Pour over vegetables; cool over medium heat, stirring gently until vegetables change color. Pack and seal. Makes about 12 pints.

Mona Ray

Heavenly Chocolate Ice Cream

12 (1 3/4 oz.) milky way bars, cut into pieces

1 (14 oz.) can sweetened condensed milk

about 3 qts. milk   1 (5.5 oz.) can chocolate syrup

Combine candy and sweetened condensed milk in a large sauce pan. Cook over low heat, stirring occasionally. Add about 1 qt. milk to candy mixture. Beat until well blended. Pour mixture into freezer can of 1 gallon freezer.

Elizabeth Walker

Homemade Sweetened Condensed Milk

1/2 c. boiling water	3 Tbsp. butter or marg.
1 1/2 c. instant dry milk	1/2 c. sugar

Yeilds 1 1/3 cups. To insure success, use boiling water and instant milk. Have the butter, sugar and milk measured and at hand. Measure the boiling water into the blender container. Add melted butter, then sugar and powdered milk. Blend once and scrape down the sides of the container. Then blend until completely smooth, about 30 seconds. Pour out and let stand until cool and thickened. Use immediatley or refrigerate covered.

Laurie Davis

Mexican Salsa

3 1/2 c. tomatoes	1 c. tomato soup
1 c. finely chopped onion	1/3 c. chopped green pepper
1/3 c. diced green chilies	1 lg. garlic clove, crushed
1 Tbsp. fresh or 1/2 dry cilantro	1/2 tsp. cumin
1/2 tsp. salt	1/4 tsp. pepper
1/2 to 1 tsp. chopped jalapeno peppers	

Mix all the preceding together in large bowl. Let stand at least 30 minutes before serving. Serve with tortilla chips.

Kelly Chaney

Quick Fudge Sundaes

1 6-oz. package (one cup) semi-sweet chocolate pieces	
1 6-oz. can evaporated milk	1/2 1-pt. jar marshmallow creme
1 pkg. vanilla ice cream	

Mix chocolate and milk in sauce pan. Heat slowly, stirring to blend. Beat in marshmallow creme till blended. Serve warm or cool over ice cream. Makes two cups.

Rena Bowser

Six Plus Three Ice Cream

3 c. whole milk	3 c. sugar
3 oranges	3 c. half and half
3 bananas	3 lemons

Mix milk, half and half and sugar together. Put in freezer and start freezing. Cut lemons and oranges in half; remove juice and pulp from fruit. Mash the bananas and mix fruits together. Mix the fruits with the milk and sugar and finish freezing.

Lena Herrington

Sweetened Condensed Milk

1 c. instant dry milk	1 1/3 c. boiling water
3 Tbsp. melted butter	2/3 c. sugar
pinch of salt	

Put in blender and blend well. This can be made ahead and kept in refrigerator.

Lorene Parvin

TABLE OF SUBSTITUTIONS

INGREDIENT	QUANTITY	SUBSTITUTE
baking powder	1 teaspoon double-acting	1½ teaspoons phosphate or tartrate or ¼ teaspoon baking soda plus ½ cup buttermilk or sour milk
butter	1 cup	1 cup margarine ⅞ to 1 cup hydrogenated fat plus ½ teaspoon salt ⅞ cup lard plus ½ teaspoon salt
chocolate	1 square unsweetened	3 tablespoons cocoa plus 1 tablespoon shortening
cream	1 cup coffee cream	3 tablespoons butter plus ⅞ cup milk
	1 cup heavy cream	1/3 cup butter plus ¾ cup milk
egg	1 whole egg	2 egg yolks
flour (for thickening)	1 tablespoon	½ tablespoon cornstarch or 2 teaspoons quick-cooking tapioca
flour	1 cup all purpose 1 cup cake flour 1 cup self-rising	1 cup plus 2 tablespoons cake flour ⅞ cup all purpose flour 1 cup flour, omit baking powder & salt
herbs	1 tablespoon fresh	1 teaspoon dried
honey	1 cup	1 to 1¼ cups sugar plus ¼ cup liquid
milk	1 cup fresh whole	1 cup reconstituted nonfat dry milk plus 2 teaspoons butter
	1 cup whole milk	½ cup evaporated milk plus ½ cup water
	1 cup sour milk	1 tablespoon lemon juice or vinegar plus sweet milk to make one cup
yeast	1 cake compressed	1 package or 2 teaspoons active dry yeast

TABLE OF EQUIVALENTS

FOOD	QUANTITY	YIELD
apples	1 medium	1 cup sliced
bread crumbs	3 to 4 slices bread	1 cup dry crumbs
	1 slice bread	¾ cup soft crumbs
cabbage	1 pound	4 cups shredded
cheese	¼ pound	1 cup shredded
cherries	1 quart	2 cups pitted
crackers, graham	15	1 cup fine crumbs
crackers, soda	16	1 cup coarse crumbs
	22	1 cup fine crumbs
cranberries	1 pound	3 to 3½ cups sauce
cream, whipping	1 cup	2 cups whipped
dried raisins, currants	1 pound	3 cups, seedless
		2½ cups, seeded
dates	1 pound	2½ cups, chopped
dry beans	1 cup	2½ cups cooked
eggs	5 medium	1 cup
	8 medium egg whites	1 cup
	12 to 14 medium egg yolks	1 cup
flour	1 pound sifted	4 cups
lemon	1	2 to 3 tablespoons juice
macaroni, spaghetti noodles	½ pound	4 cups cooked
nuts, peanuts	5 ounces	1 cup
pecans, chopped	4¼ ounces	1 cup
halves	3¾ ounces	1 cup
walnuts, chopped	4½ ounces	1 cup
halves	3½ ounces	1 cup
onion	1 medium	½ cup chopped
orange	1	1/3 to 1/2 cup juice
rice	1 cup	3½ cups cooked
rice, precooked	1 cup	2 cups cooked
sugar, brown	1 pound	2¼ cups firmly packed
confectioners'	1 pound	3½ cups sifted
granulated	1 pound	2¼ cups

THE MOST USUAL
WEIGHTS AND MEASURES

A pinch	=	⅛ teaspoon or less
1 tablespoon	=	3 teaspoons
4 tablespoons	=	¼ cup
8 tablespoons	=	½ cup
12 tablespoons	=	¾ cup
1 cup of liquid	=	½ pint
2 cups of liquid	=	1 pint
4 cups of liquid	=	1 quart
2 pints of liquid	=	1 quart
4 quarts	=	1 gallon
8 quarts	=	1 peck, such as apples, pears, etc.
16 ounces	=	1 pound

INDEX OF RECIPES

Produced by Trimble Publishing Company
Hardy, Arkansas

Order a book for a friend ...
It's a Perfect Gift!

ORDER FORM

For additional copies of the *Evening Shade* Cookbook write:

Evening Shade School Foundation
P.O. Box 36
Evening Shade, AR 72532
Telephone: 1-800-545-4825   Fax: 1-501-266-3657

Please mail me _____ copies of the *Evening Shade* Cookbook at $7.00 per copy, postage-paid, for each book. Enclosed is my check for $ _____ .

Mail books to:

Name_____

Address_____

City_____State_____Zip_____

Mail to: Evening Shade School Foundation, P.O. Box 36, Evening Shade, AR 72532

Please mail me _____ copies of the *Evening Shade* Cookbook at $7.00 per copy, postage-paid, for each book. Enclosed is my check for $ _____ .

Mail books to:

Name_____

Address_____

City_____State_____Zip_____

Mail to: Evening Shade School Foundation, P.O. Box 36, Evening Shade, AR 72532

Burt Knows Evening Shade **T-Shirts**
ORDER FORM

Evening Shade School Foundation • P.O. Box 36 • Evening Shade, AR 72532
Telephone: 1-800-545-4825   Fax: 1-501-266-3657

Please mail me _____ "Burt Knows" Evening Shade, Arkansas

Tee Shirts at $10.00, postage-paid, for each Tee Shirt.

Enclosed is my check for $_____ .

Please circle adult size: Small   Medium   Large   X-Large   XX-Large

Mail Tee Shirts to:

Name_____

Address_____

City_____State_____Zip_____

Mail to: Evening Shade School Foundation, P.O. Box 36, Evening Shade, Arkansas 72532

Evening Shade License T-Shirts
ORDER FORM

Evening Shade School Foundation • P.O. Box 36 • Evening Shade, AR 72532
Telephone: 1-800-545-4825   Fax: 1-501-266-3657

Please mail me _____ Evening Shade, Arkansas License Plate

Tee Shirts at $10.00, postage-paid, for each Tee Shirt.

Enclosed is my check for $_____ .

Please circle adult size: Small   Medium   Large   X-Large   XX-Large

Mail Tee Shirts to:

Name_____

Address_____

City_____State_____Zip_____

Mail to: Evening Shade School Foundation, P.O. Box 36, Evening Shade, Arkansas 72532